D1549354

developing
interactive skills

developing
INTERACTIVE SKILLS

Neil Rackham
Peter Honey
Michael J Colbert
Ray Fields
Derek Hinson
Terry Morgan
Michael Morris
Roger Sugden
Stephen Tribe

Wellens Publishing

WELLENS PUBLISHING
The Sun, Guilsborough, Northampton NN6 8PY, England

First published in Great Britain 1971

ISBN 903084 00 7

Designed by Eric Sweet

Printed in Great Britain by The Leagrave Press Limited,
Mount Pleasant Road, Luton LU3 2RS

contents

preface
JOHN WELLENS

page 1 **chapter 1**
a critical survey of training in interactive skills
TERRY MORGAN

46 **chapter 2**
the search for new methods in interactive skills training
NEIL RACKHAM

68 **chapter 3**
interface behaviour and organisational effectiveness
NEIL RACKHAM   PETER HONEY   ROGER SUGDEN

92 **chapter 4**
collecting behavioural data
MICHAEL J COLBERT   MICHAEL MORRIS   STEPHEN TRIBE

118 **chapter 5**
feeding back behavioural data
PETER HONEY   RAY FIELDS   DEREK HINSON

143 **chapter 6**
mixing – a new technique in training
NEIL RACKHAM

161 **chapter 7**
the trainer's guide to successful plagiarism
PETER HONEY

183 biographies

187 advertisement

188 index

contents

preface
john walker

page 1 chapter 1

chapter 2

60 chapter 3

92 chapter 4

118 chapter 5

143 chapter 6

161 chapter 7

183

187 advertisements

189 index

figures

page 60 **1** typical interactive skills course design
61 **2** the trainer functions in interactive skills training
62 **3** splitting the trainer functions
64 **4** a model for interactive skills training
81 **5** applicability of training to different parts of the organisation
82 **6** job knowledge cluster UK
82 **7** job knowledge cluster USA and Canada
83 **8** strict/critical cluster USA
97 **9** recording conversation
99 **10** behaviour analysis ICL
103 **11** behaviour analysis BOAC
114 **12** behaviour analysis training in BOAC
122 **13** BOAC individual data record sheet
124 **14** data summary BOAC
126 **15** data collapse printout ICL
128 **16** the individual behaviour summary
129 **17** ICL management training session assessment
136 **18** BOAC – development of supervisory skills course
138 **19** behaviour aims worksheet
150 **20** how a contribution rate mix works
151 **21** changes in contribution rate caused by mixing groups
153 **22** changes in contribution rate in an ICL two group course
155 **23** behaviour category breakdown of ICL contribution rate mix
158 **24** general effect of negative behaviour mixes
175 **25** histogram display
176 **26** behaviour ratios

Preface
John Wellens

This book is an account of developments in the field of
man-management which have taken place within the past three
years in two British companies – BOAC and International
Computers Ltd. It is, essentially, a case study of the way in which
these two companies developed some of their ideas over this
period of time. Following this early developmental work the team
has built up further experience in several other companies in
Britain and abroad.

Training managers to be more effective in group situations, or to be
more concerned with the inter-relationships between members of a
working group or to improve the effectiveness of the boss-
subordinate relationship is not new. This interest has gradually
come to the fore in management training over the past fifteen
years or so, particularly in the United States where the actual
volume of effort has been considerable.

The study reported in this book started in 1968. Peter Honey and
his colleagues were trying to find more effective techniques for
developing the interactive skills of BOAC personnel – the supervisors
particularly. At that time there was a growing feeling in the
training business that knowledge-oriented courses of all sorts were
deceptively ineffective or, if not ineffective, seriously limited. Their
limitations in the field of adapting human behaviour in the working
group was beginning to be accepted. This recognition started off a
search for improved methods based on more effective learning
situations which, ideally, would move well away from formal
lecturing as the basic technique.

It was to this problem of creating meaningful learning situations in
this field that Honey and his BOAC colleagues addressed themselves
under the overall direction of Mike Colbert, BOAC's manager of
general training. Honey, himself a psychologist working in the field
of management training, drew in the services of Neil Rackham, a
psychologist working in the research field. Rackham had already
carried out research into evaluation of training methods and the
intention of BOAC was to use Rackham's expertise and experience
in evaluating any new methods tried out by Honey and his
colleagues. The work was seen to be important, so much so that it
attracted the support of the Air Transport and Travel Industry
Training Board who provided research funds for its development.
During the course of the research and development study Peter
Honey moved to ICL to carry out similar work in that company

Preface

and this added a new dimension in that the concepts had to be adapted to a new environment.

Thus was born a highly experimental team of vigorous young men, some university-based, some industry-based, some research-based and others oriented towards training. This book records their thoughts, their ambitions and their accomplishments. Their intention was to produce more effective learning situations and to avoid, wherever possible, chalk and talk. A large part of their purpose was to measure behaviour change and thus to exercise some control over it. One of their achievements has been to bring a more analytical approach to management behaviour itself. Earlier studies of behaviour in the work situation tend to treat it in the macro-fashion: for instance, the participative style of management is one of these macro-descriptions of behaviour. By contrast this DIS team deals with behaviour in a more micro-fashion, breaking down behaviour patterns into behavioural elements. This in itself makes the subject more amenable to study and experiment and, eventually, to control.

The study is still continuing. What the team has accomplished is the opening up of an important field to further development through the use of a particular battery of techniques, some of which existed already and some of which they invented or modified. Behaviour analysis, for example, is not new but the use made of the data, particularly the use of mixing techniques, brings something new and valuable.

Of the importance of this field of study and its application there can be no doubt. Besides the pressures exerted by the need for increasing the efficiency of organisations, the pressure of the social and political situations in most countries will re-angle thoughts towards human beings and their real needs and the way they might be satisfied in social and work groups. The desire for a more open and participative style of management will exert pressures of its own.

If this book does no more than excite people to think more actively and positively about behaviour it will have achieved its purpose.

developing
interactive skills

a critical survey
of training in

TERRY MORGAN
Research Adviser
Air Transport and Travel ITB

'The trouble with Fred is that he seems to
rub everyone up the wrong way. No wonder
he's always complaining he doesn't get any
co-operation.'
'My boss is never willing to listen to my
ideas. There's always some excuse for
putting me off till another time.'
'Well, he might be the man for the job, but
I just couldn't say. Half-an-hour's interview,
and I hardly got a thing out of him.'
'I can't understand these subordinates of
mine. Sure, they seem to hit it off well
enough with each other – you would think
they would make a first-class team. But they
never seem to get things done on time.'

2 a critical survey of training in interactive skills

FEW PEOPLE CAN HAVE WORKED IN AN ORGANISATION FOR ANY length of time without hearing, or perhaps even expressing, comments like these. Human relations: the oil that keeps the organisational wheels turning – or, more often it seems, the grit that makes the machine shudder.

Human relations problems in organisations are as old as the time when man discovered that if he wanted to do certain things he would have to work on them with others. However, it is only in very recent years – in rough terms, the last 40 – that these problems have been systematically studied and described using the methods of the infant sciences of psychology and sociology.

Side-by-side with these scientific studies, which are slowly dissolving our ignorance of how men work together and why they don't work together better, has grown an interest and concern on the part of practical men of affairs with the human factor in organisations. It has increasingly come to be recognised that people are a key resource of the organisation, who can make the difference between a just respectable balance on the company accounts and a healthy, glowing profit. 'Better management of human resources!' is the slogan shouted today from a myriad of seminar brochures and conference platforms. 'Unlock the creative potential of your staff!' 'Motivate your unwilling workers!' 'Make the powerful forces inherent in the group work for the organisation, not against it!' And so on.

But how? How do we deal with these irritating human relations problems that so often hamper individuals, groups and even whole organisations from pursuing the job they are paid to do, or exist to do? Why does Fred not get on with his fellow managers? Why is Bill a poor boss, and Harry a hopeless interviewer? Why do work groups fail to achieve satisfactorily the tasks they have been set?

Psychology, now perhaps well on its way to adolescence, is able to give us some very elaborate and plausible explanations, based on a great deal of careful study of what happens when one person interacts with another, or when a group of people interact together. It is also able to offer suggestions on how to get better bosses and interviewers, for example, or how to get more out of work groups. Many of these suggestions have been tried and developed, with mixed success let it be admitted, but on balance probably more success than failure. It is largely the purpose of this book to describe and examine some of the ways of helping people to deal with other people that have proved to be reasonably successful.

Human relations problems, essentially, are *dealing with people* problems. In the work organisation, they are the problems of boss dealing with subordinates, of members of teams or committees dealing with each other, of inter-viewer dealing with interviewee, and of trainer dealing with trainee.

You do not need to be a psychologist to observe that some individuals are obviously more adept than others at dealing with people. They are better able to get their way without engendering hostility; others are willing to tell them things, and also to listen to them; they are better at calming troubled waters, or drawing out more effort from individuals or groups. The question we are interested in is, why?

We are used to explaining why some people are better than others at certain things either in terms of what they are (their intelligence, aptitudes, personality, interests, attitudes), or of what they know, or of what they do (skills). In the case of dealing with people, we will postulate that some individuals are more successful than others because they are more **skilled,** that is, they either do certain things that others do not, or they do them better. This is not the whole truth, of course; some of the differences are almost certainly due to aptitudes and personality factors. However, from the point of view of helping people to deal with others more success-fully, it is the skill explanation which is the important one, because skills can be developed, whereas aptitudes and personality are relatively stable in the adult and not very susceptible to modification. Knowledge may also be a factor, but since dealing with people involves doing – ie skill, there is obviously more justification in attributing **The lesson** differences between individuals to what they do than to **that knowing is** what they know. The lesson that *knowing is not doing* has **not doing has taken a** taken a long time to learn, but it is now well recog ised. **long time to learn** Although our suggestion that individual differences in

4 a critical survey of training in interactive skills

success at *dealing with people* problems can most profitably, from the point of view of training, be attributed to skills, we should note that not everyone would agree. There is a respectable body of opinion that believes these differences are largely a matter of values and attitudes. Now values and attitudes, which we often regard as one reflection of an individual's personality, **can** be modified by training, even though they resist change fairly strongly. The argument is, therefore, that the road to improving the ways in which individuals deal with others is through attitude change: get the attitudes right, and the desired behaviours (skills) will automatically follow.

It will not be denied that attitudes intervene in the inter-actions between people, or that they influence behaviour. Nor, at this stage, will we pursue the relative merits of concentrating on behaviour change or on attitude change in order to improve the facility to deal with others. We shall be in a better position to do this after we have considered what happens when one person interacts with another. For the time being we will accept the postulate that skills, which are learnable, are the most important contributors to differences in the facility to deal with people.

INTERACTIVE SKILLS

The question that immediately follows is, what are these skills? The short answer is that they are INTERACTIVE SKILLS. (Variants on this label* include human relations skills, social skills and interpersonal skills.) However, this does not take us very far. Can we describe what we mean by inter-active skills? We can, although as Michael Argyle has pointed out, it is by no means easy. He says

Social interaction is a fascinating and baffling object of study: on the one hand it is immediate and familiar, on the other it is mysterious and inexpressible – there do not seem to be the words to describe it, or the concepts to handle it.

In spite of this seemingly pessimistic statement, Argyle has in fact done much to increase our understanding of the

* *The choice of label is a matter of personal preference rather than anything more significant. My colleagues who are contributing to this book prefer INTERACTIVE SKILLS to the other variants, and there is merit in consistency.*

nature and operation of interactive skills. Anyone who is interested in following up this subject in much greater depth than can be attempted in this chapter, is referred to his very readable book on interpersonal behaviour[1].

A useful starting point is to ask what we are doing when we interact with others. This will help us to understand what interactive skills are, although it will not tell us how we perform them. At one level, we can say that we are, for example, talking – ie indulging in verbal behaviour – asking questions, making statements, giving instructions and so on. Or, we may be nodding, smiling, laughing, looking someone in the eye, or making physical contact – shaking hands, clapping on the shoulder, kissing, for example. Verbal behaviour is probably the thing we notice most when people are interacting together, but the non-verbal behaviours are very important adjuncts. All these things are observable, and clearly they are a part of what we mean by interactive skills. However, description of what is going on at this level does not take us far enough. Behaviours of the kinds mentioned can best be regarded as the bricks of interactive skills – the components from which the skills are built up. Argyle calls them SOCIAL TECHNIQUES.

At a higher level, we can describe interactions in terms of what the participants are trying to achieve. That is, we introduce the notion of purpose, or objectives. This accords with our commonsense ideas about skills, which include the concept of behaviour directed towards some end or other. Thus, a person is not merely talking to a group of others, but he is teaching them, or enlisting their co-operation. It is possible to think of a whole variety of purposes for which people interact with others: we have already mentioned two that occur in work organisations; others would include eliciting information about a job applicant, disciplining a subordinate, and obtaining a decision from a committee. These are some of the kinds of things we do when we deal with other people at work and we may suggest that the patterns of behaviour used in doing these things are our interactive skills.

This approach seems to point to the fact that we are right to talk of interactive skills in the plural. An interesting

B

6 a critical survey of training in interactive skills

question which follows is whether it is possible to classify interactive skills – ie whether they can be grouped together on the basis of similarities, or arranged in some kind of hierarchy as aptitudes can be. The findings in relation to other kinds of human attributes would lead us to expect that a classification could be constructed, but to the best of my knowledge there is at present no widely accepted taxonomy of interactive skills. It would seem, however, that a description of interactive skills in terms of what they are directed towards is both meaningful and practically useful. Further, for the time being we must be content with just being able to describe and name interactive skills. Doubtless, research will take us before long to the next step, where we can work with a classification.

So far, we have dealt in a rather cursory fashion with what interactive skills are, and have identified a number of skills (which is by no means exhaustive) in terms of the purposes for which people interact with others. In passing, and just to make the picture a little more complete, we may note that the objectives mentioned above have in common the fact they they are external to our hypothetical interactive skills operator. Another set of objectives which people can be seeking to achieve in their interactions with others are internal ones: that is, they relate to the personal needs of the operator. Argyle, in the book quoted from earlier, refers to these personal needs as social drives, or motivators, and he lists seven, which include such things as affiliation – the need for acceptance by peers and groups of peers; dominance – the need to be deferred to; and self-esteem and ego-identity – the need to have others accept one's self-image as valid. In most interactive situations where the main objective is external, a person will also be using his skills to achieve one or more of the internal objectives. Thus, for example, a trainer may not only be concerned with getting his charges to learn, but also with impressing them – the self-esteem drive; a member of a work group may be concerned both to influence the group to take a certain action, and to be liked and accepted by his fellow members. Often, the external and internal objectives will be in conflict. We must now move on to examine how interactive skills are performed. Again, the necessity to try to be brief unfortunately does not permit the treatment that the matter warrants. We have already referred to the behaviours, verbal and otherwise, that play a part in interactive skills. But the behaviours themselves are far from being the sole constituents of the skill performance: they are simply the observable aspects.

But the behaviours themselves are far from being the sole constituents of the skill performance: they are simply the observable aspects

The kinds of process that enter into the performance of interactive skills are common to all these skills, whatever the objective to which they are directed. Perhaps the best way of looking at them is to follow through an imaginary dyad interaction, ie one involving just two persons, between two characters whom we will impersonally style A and B, considering in general terms the processes that are at work. Group interactions are rather more complex, because one person can be dealing with several persons simultaneously, but most of what we can learn from the dyad interaction is also relevant to groups.

We will make certain assumptions: that A has initiated the interaction, and is primarily seeking to achieve an objective with respect to B that is external to his personal needs. The objective we will leave unspecified. The first important thing we note from A's point of view is that B is another person, not a machine, or a set of figures. Now because B is a person he will have objectives of his own, one of which initially may well be to avoid having anything to do with A, let alone to allow A to achieve his own objective with respect to B. Also, B will certainly not be inert and passive – it is after all an interactive situation; he will produce behaviours, and A has to take account of these.

A will seek, in the interaction, to order his behaviour in a way he believes will be suited to the objective he wishes to achieve. However, unless he is lucky, he will not be able to start off immediately in pursuit of that objective. He must first of all achieve the sub-objective of bringing B into play – that is, he must make sure that B will accede to interacting with A. Now, an interesting point is that the way A sets about developing his interaction with B depends on factors other than the objective A has in view. Most importantly, it will be influenced by how A sees, or perceives, B and by

8 a critical survey
of training in
interactive skills

what he knows about B. In other words, B is a source of stimuli for A, and part of the explanation of the way A behaves towards B lies in the stimuli (cues) he receives from B, and how he interprets them.

The mechanisms that are at work are complex, but we now understand quite a lot about them. Let's pick out the main ones. A will have certain impressions of B, and these will trigger attitudes and feelings towards B. A may already have had some acquaintance with B, and therefore know things about him. What he knows may or may not be accurate. His attitudes towards B will be partly dependent on this knowledge he has of B, but they will probably also be affected by deeper-rooted attitudes that A has about, for example, people in general, or people with characteristics similar to B's. These attitudes will affect, in turn, A's choice of behaviours (in fact, will probably limit the range of behaviours he draws on), and the way he sequences them.

A may of course be meeting B for the first time. He will nevertheless, unless he is abnormal, quickly form impressions of B and adopt attitudes towards him which will largely be based on those he has towards groups of people to whom B appears to have similarities. Nothing is going to stop A, or anyone else, from adopting attitudes towards another; what is important is their appropriateness. It seems that the appropriateness or otherwise of other-directed attitudes is affected to a considerable extent by what is technically labelled social sensitivity or empathy. Whatever else this attribute is, it seems to involve the ability to make finer discriminations between people, to receive and correctly interpret a wider range of cues from others and generally, to be more accurate in assessing another's feelings and attitudes. Social sensitivity is of course an important factor throughout A's interaction with B, in so far as it influences the extent to which A is open to B and is able to modify his attitudes and his behaviours to ensure that the desired outcome of the interaction is achieved. There is some evidence that social sensitivity is improvable by training and it would seem appropriate to regard it as an integral part of interactive skills.

There is some evidence that social sensitivity is improvable by training and it would seem appropriate to regard it as an integral part of interactive skills

We have already mentioned that A's attitudes towards B

exercise a limiting effect on the behaviours which he will choose to build up his interactively skilled performance. If he strongly dislikes B, he may find it impossible to smile at him in a warm manner, for instance, although smiling is certainly part of A's normal repertoire of behaviours. On the other hand, if B is female and attractive, A will find it hard to refrain from giving her obvious appraising looks! But in addition to dictating the behaviours available to A, it is important to note that his attitudes also act as a filter for the cues that B is emitting during their interaction. A will tend to see only those things which reinforce his attitudes, and this may seriously reduce the likelihood of achieving his objective. Attitudes towards B, in other words, influence both the receptor and the motor parts of A's interactive skill process.

We still have not said all there is about attitudes, beliefs and values. We have so far talked about A's attitudes towards B, but these are not the only ones that will influence A's performance. For example, A's attitudes towards himself, or his role in relation to B, will cause him to regard certain behaviours as *not quite the thing to do*, and therefore to be avoided. Or again, he may hold values or beliefs that put some behaviours out of court, even though he can see that they could help him to achieve his objective. Thus, his knowledge of B may suggest that a dirty story would be just the technique to bring B into play initially, but if A has had a rigidly puritan upbringing, and has internalised the values, he is most unlikely to bring himself to use that particular technique. As a last example, A may also hold beliefs about best ways of achieving the objective he has in view, and this will clearly prescribe the behaviours he incorporates into his performance, regardless of who or what B is. Thus, if his objective is to get B to mend his ways – perhaps to get to work on time – and he believes that this kind of objective can only be achieved by instilling fear into people – we could predict fairly well the nature of the behaviours A will employ.

The rather simple description given above of how interactive skills work has laid considerable emphasis on the role played by attitudes, beliefs and values in their performance.

10 a critical survey of training in interactive skills

Attitudes are important as determinants of the behaviours a person will use in a situation with a given objective. Achieving interactive objectives is largely a matter of selecting appropriate behaviours, but it seems that it is not sufficient that a person has the appropriate behaviours in his repertoire. They also have to be available to him – ie he must be able to select them as appropriate, and attitudes, we have suggested, may be an inhibiting influence.

The performance of interactive skills, then, does depend on what a person is, as reflected in his attitudes. Or, we can put it that what a person does when he is dealing with others, ie exercising interactive skills, is determined by what his attitudes let him do. The interplay of a person's make-up with what he does is not by any means peculiar to the interactive skills area, although it is probably more important in this area simply because working with people is a very different proposition from working with, say, things or data. In the light of the rudimentary analysis of an interactive situation that has been presented, it is easy to understand why many people consider that the way to improve interactive skills is to change attitudes. Some of the methods that have been developed for training these skills are based on this theory. Two things must be allowed: first, it has been demonstrated quite clearly that attitudes **can** be changed; second, attitude change **has** been shown to issue in behaviour change. However, the evidence for the latter is nowhere near as compelling as for the former. In many cases where changes of attitude have been achieved, behavioural effects, other than verbalising the attitudes, have not been satisfactorily demonstrated. Furthermore, in those cases where they have, the related behavioural change has often only been of a fairly gross kind – such as a change of shopping habits – not involving any skill as such.

We may ask why we should expect a changed attitude to have a beneficial effect on a skill Indeed, we may ask why we should expect a changed attitude to have a beneficial effect on a skill. Certainly it may facilitate the use of behaviours required to build up the skill, but unless the skill itself has been demonstrated to the person, and he has had the chance to practise it, we should be justifiably surprised to see an improvement in skill. We must remember that the behaviours associated with the old attitudes have probably been firmly established by experience and long use, and to replace them may require substantial unlearning and rebuilding.

An example may help. Let us take a manager whose attitude to his staff has been that they are unwilling workers, reluctant to take any responsibility, and that they require a close watch to be maintained over them to be kept up to the mark. Consistent with his attitude, the manager has generally made decisions himself, given orders to the staff, and checked their work frequently to ensure that his instructions were being carried out. As a result of training, the manager's attitude changes. He now takes the view that his staff are self-motivating, desire responsibility, wish to participate in decision-making and can be left to get on with a job by themselves. We would expect the manager's behaviour to change from its former authoritarian style to a participative one. We would in fact probably observe some changes, but we would very likely be disappointed if we expected to observe the manager displaying skills in, for example, group decision-making. It is not enough that he should want to behave in this way; he has to know how to, and to have practised doing it.

We may note one other problem associated with the approach that relies on attitude change as the means of improving interactive skills. It is that identifying the specific attitudes that need to be modified in order to improve a particular interactive skill, is a very difficult task. When considering our hypothetical interaction between characters A and B earlier, we saw that a variety of attitudes could be influencing A's perceptions of B, and his behaviours towards B. In a real situation, it would be a daunting prospect to have to investigate the complex of attitudes possessed by even one person which could potentially affect his interactions with others, and to set about modifying them. Moreover, attitudes, because they are a part of a person's make-up, are very personal. If we are trying to improve the interactive skills of a group of people, using the attitude change approach, we would virtually have to have an individual programme for each person. While individualised instruction is perhaps an ideal for any kind of training, in this instance it would

**12 a critical survey
of training in
interactive skills**

hardly be practicable, and would not use resources efficiently. While not denying the role of attitudes, or the complexities of their interplay with behaviour in interactive situations, the case that has emerged for approaching the development of interactive skills directly through behaviour change is clearly a strong one. The main point in its favour is that dealing with people does involve behaviour – doing – and if we want to modify behaviours, people must have a chance to try out and practice the new ones required by the skills into which they have to be integrated. It may be asked, in view of all that has gone before, whether new behaviours and skills developed in a training situation are likely to be maintained if attitudes have been ignored. Interestingly, it does appear from several research studies that behaviour changes actually induce attitude changes in some cases. It seems that the practice of new behaviours, accompanied by success in achieving the objectives of interactive situations, causes attitudes to be modified so as to bring about congruence with the results of the behavioural experimentation. Such findings are a further illustration of the very close link between attitudes and behaviour; they also vindicate the choice of behaviour change as the target in trying to develop interactive skills.

Having considered the nature of interactive skills in some detail, we can now move on to examine some of the methods that are available for assisting people to deal with others more effectively. Our concern will be mainly with more recent developments in this field. The training methods that will be described can all claim some measure of success in improving interactive skills. The fact that they are thriving is evidence of a kind that they satisfy the needs of at least some people. However, one could wish, in every case, that they had been subjected to more rigorous evaluation than has occurred to date. The very high level of demand for such training, taken together with the fact that almost any new development in the field can be guaranteed an enthusiastic response, are not conditions conducive to a concern with evaluation. Most of the methods can be criticised on one point or another and some indeed have been subjected to extremely strong criticism. The criticisms ought to stimulate more research into the dynamics of the methods and the results they achieve.

On one or two of the methods, there is already a voluminous literature, descriptive, analytical, and (at least quasi-) evaluative. In the short space of this chapter, adequate justice cannot be done to the methods, but references are given so that anyone not too familiar with them can follow-up some of the literature to get a fuller picture. Also, no attempt has been made to include every interactive skills training method that is currently in vogue. Those covered represent what appear to be the main lines of development. Collectively, they probably illustrate also the main problems of interactive skills training.

Before looking at specific training methods we should perhaps consider what features we would expect to find in any method that aims to improve interactive skills. One we have already stressed, namely that the method should almost certainly contain the opportunity to experiment with behaviours and to practice the skills which it is seeking to develop. This is a condition for learning any skill, in fact. You do not learn to swim, to play tennis, to drive a motor car or to make love simply by reading books or being told; to do these things, and especially to become competent at them, they have to be practised. A second, and inseparable condition if improvement is to be effected, is that the skill operator must receive feedback on how well he is doing. One of the reasons why many people are not very good at dealing with others is that little or no feedback was given to, or obtained by, them when they were acquiring, through the usual channel of unguided experience, the behaviour patterns that they now use. The role of feedback in learning is familiar to all trainers, and many lay-persons; unfortunately, the difficulty the learner has in abstracting feedback from a situation, and especially those of an interactive kind, is not always adequately recognised.

We might also reasonably expect that an interactive skills training method would be soundly based on discovery learning principles. To some extent this is assured if the training allows for experiment and practice of behaviours. However, because of the close link between attitudes and

If improvement is to be effected, the skill operator must receive feedback on how well he is doing

**14 a critical survey
of training in
interactive skills**

interactive skills, and because of the very strength of the
habits of behaviour that the training is attempting to modify,
learning theory would suggest that success is more likely if
the trainee is helped to discover for himself the inappropriate-
ness of his established behaviours. He will then be more
strongly motivated to seek more appropriate ones, and to
continue to use them when he leaves the training situation.
One can confidently assert that the foregoing conditions are
essential if any permanent improvement in interactive skills
is to be brought about. There are two others which can be
mentioned as probably desirable, although this could be
argued over. The first is that the interactive situations used
for training purposes, in which the skills will be practised,
should be as real as possible. It is not often feasible to use an
actual on-the-job situation, unless all the parties to the
interaction are being trained, because of the risks involved
in experimenting with new behaviours. That being so, the
training simulations should be as relevant to the actual skills
that are being trained as possible. We have already noted
that there seem to be a variety of interactive skills, definable
in terms principally of their objectives, and we do not know
enough about them yet to say to what extent they contain
common elements, and to what extent the skills are specific.
We might note Argyle's[1] comment that *it is not known
whether or not there is a general factor of social competence* and
agree with him that *there is probably some generality about social
competence, because certain of the elements of skill – for example
social sensitivity – are needed in all social situations.* However,
until we know more, it would seem wisest to assume that
specific aspects of interactive skills require closely simulated
situations for their improvement. In simple terms, if we want
to improve information – eliciting skill (interviewing), then
simulated interviews should probably be the primary
training medium.
The second possibly desirable condition is that trainees
should be given knowledge relevant to the problems of
dealing with people, so that they can work out why the ways
in which they are learning to behave are more successful
than other ways. This suggestion is more controversial,
because there has been in recent years something of a

reaction against knowledge – based training. The reaction has been perhaps rather undiscriminating: while the merits of 'learning by doing' cannot be disputed it may be that the baby has gone with the bath water. It should be remembered that one acceptable definition of skill is *applied knowledge* and for some skills, amongst which we should put interactive ones, sufficient knowledge to allow conceptualisation of what is going on in the skill performance is probably very important for effectiveness. Also, it may reasonably be hypothesised that giving trainees some of the theory of interactive behaviour will assist in the process of generalising their skills, particularly from the training to the work situation, and in using their subsequent interactive experiences to further their learning.

Much of the early work in the field of interactive skills training was firmly based on the notion that it is sufficient to give people knowledge about social interaction and interpersonal phenomena in order to make them better able to handle interactive situations. The methods used to give the knowledge might be lectures, discussions or case-studies, the latter generally finding more favour, because on the whole they tend to result in better learning. We may note that the knowledge-based approach to teaching interactive skills is still very widespread. Many management and supervisory training programmes are constructed entirely around the methods mentioned, and aim to do no more than impart knowledge; it must be presumed that those who construct the courses believe that increased knowledge will result in improved interactive skills. There is no evidence that they do, which makes it all the more surprising that such approaches are still persisted with. One good reason for their continuing popularity may be that participants usually find them interesting and enjoyable, and rate them, if they are asked, as highly relevant to their jobs. Such results are very reinforcing for the trainer. Another reason is that this approach to human relations training is much the easiest option open to the trainer. The newer approaches, which we shall examine in a moment, demand trainer skills which are still in very short supply. If the trainer must attempt something, but is not competent to handle the newer methods, it is inevitable that the traditional ones will be used. We should not scorn the latter completely however; they do some good, and are better than nothing. They certainly improve knowledge of interactive processes, and may increase social sensitivity which we have already referred to as an important aspect of interactive skills. Group discussions and case-studies have also been shown to bring about attitude changes.

ROLE-PLAYING

While we are on the subject of traditional approaches to interactive skills training, it is right that we should mention another one that is not only long-established but has also been demonstrated to be very successful in improving certain interactive skills. It is the well-known method of role-playing, or psycho-drama. It is not infrequently used along with the methods described in the previous paragraph, and in its most common form will involve two participants who will be observed by the remainder of the training group and the trainer. There is little need to describe the method in any detail. The participants are usually carefully briefed on the roles they are to play, and on the context of their interaction; they then spontaneously act out the situation according to the way they think the persons whose roles they are taking would behave. Typical role-play situations might involve a salesman and a difficult customer, an interviewer and a job applicant, or a boss and subordinate. A variant on the dyad interaction is MULTIPLE ROLE-PLAYING, described by Maier and Zerfoss[2], where trainees are grouped into small teams, and each member is given instructions to play a particular role.

The method meets to a greater or lesser degree most of the conditions we stipulated earlier for effective interactive skills training. It allows the participants to try out new behaviours. Feedback can be given immediately after the role-play by the trainer, and also by other trainees who have been observing. It is even possible to give feedback during role-play, if the participants wear an earphone through which the trainer can whisper comments and instructions. The subjective feedback of observers can easily be augmented by recording the interaction (tape or video) for the participants to hear or see afterwards. The trainees are most certainly actively involved in the learning process, and there is scope for discovery learning, although the extent to which it is exploited will be dependent on the trainer. Solem[3], in a paper which compares the case-study approach with role-playing, distinguishes the characteristics of the latter as follows

ROLE-PLAYING
● places the problem, the subject of the role-play, in a life-like setting
● involves problems with ongoing processes
● typically deals with problems involving the participants themselves
● deals with emotional and attitudinal aspects in an experimental frame of reference
● emphasises the importance of feelings
● deals with participants who are psychologically inside the problem situation
● makes for emotional involvement
● provides practice in interpersonal skills
● provides for testing ideas and hypotheses
● trains in emotional control
● provides for execution of the action or solution
● involves continuous feedback

Follow-up studies of role-play training have shown that it makes participants more sensitive to interpersonal pheno-mena, and more accurate in perceiving their own behaviour. It modifies attitudes, and assists the development of inter-active skills.

The method does have drawbacks. It appears that the amount of learning depends on the context in which the role-playing takes place. The technique is sometimes resented by trainees as childish. Participants may overact their parts, and put more emphasis on acting than problem-solving. Feedback may be irrelevant, as for example, if approval is given for the acting rather than for insight into the problem. Observers, who may not have the chance to be participants, are not exposed to an equivalent learning experience. And finally, the method seems to be much more suited to training the interactive skills required by dyad interactions than those demanded in group work.

18 a critical survey of training in interactive skills

THE GROUP METHOD

This last point provides a good lead-in to our consideration of more recent developments in interactive skills training, all of which are based on what we may call THE GROUP METHOD. That is, they use small groups as the primary vehicle of learning, and they are designed mainly **to help people to function more effectively in groups, and to assist the group itself to work more effectively.** Their protagonists would probably also claim that they lead to individual learning relevant to the skills required in dyad interactions, even though this is not their main orientation. Before we examine some of the methods in more detail, we might consider this characteristic that they obviously have in common, and which possibly outweighs the differences in their emphasis. What has provided the impetus for, and justification of, the small-group approach to interactive skills training? Two main factors will be suggested.

The first is the recognition, by social and occupational psychologists, by sociologists and organisation theorists, and more recently by managers themselves, of the pervasiveness and importance of groups to organisational functioning. An organisation is not so much a collection of individuals, as a complicated interlocking system of groups, each of which can have almost a life of its own. The awareness of the important role of groups, especially informal ones, can be traced back to the famous HAWTHORNE STUDIES, carried out by Harvard social scientists in a plant of the Western Electric Company in the 1930's. It came to be realised that groups within the organisation were an important source of personal satisfaction, particularly of social needs, for individuals; that groups exerted strong social pressures on their members which were a significant influence on behaviour at work; and that informal groups were often a means of protecting individual interests: a medium for resisting change. Groups were also the primary medium for accomplishing many kinds of work, a primacy that has increased as organisations have expanded, diversified, and developed ever more specialisation of function. Productivity depended on the morale of groups, on group effort and effectiveness.

Understanding group processes, and learning how to work with and through groups, therefore came to be seen as a vital requirement for supervisors and managers at all levels. While it is true that the manager is responsible for the work of individuals, and depends on them for the successful accomplishment of his own objectives, it is also the case that results are achieved more often th.. n not through groups. Group life impinges on the manage.'s work in two main ways. First, his subordinates often form a group, which he must work through, influence, and lead. Although in a sense a member of that group, he has a defined role in relation to its members. Second, the manager will usually also be a member of a peer group, containing managers at a similar level in the organisation, and from time to time he may be a member of a range of other groups convened for special purposes. Such groups will often be important for achieving organisation objectives; the manager's role in them will be more flexible, less clearly defined, and he has to find appropriate ways of integrating in the group, of working effectively with his colleagues, so that the group's goals are achieved. Alongside, and indeed out of, the growth of insight into the nature, role and functions of groups in organisations has also come new understanding of the nature of leadership itself, in particular the notion that the appropriate kind of leadership depends on situational factors, and that within a group, leadership is a function of group task, and the stage of group development.

The second factor that has contributed to the rise of small-group training methods has been recognition of the potency of the group as a medium for modifying and changing individual attitudes and values. This recognition can be traced back to the early work and theories of the American psychologist, Kurt Lewin, and owes much of its later development to the subsequent activities of the Research Center for Group Dynamics. This centre, which was originally at MIT, then at the Institute for Social Research, University of Michigan, was established by Lewin in 1945. Out of the research into the dynamics of small groups has come an understanding of how groups develop, norms evolve, and cohesiveness is built up. Research has also

The potency of the group as a medium for modifying and changing individual attitudes and values

**20 a critical survey
of training in
interactive skills**

shown the extent to which a strong, cohesive group can control aspects of a member's behaviour traditionally thought to be expressive of enduring personality traits. For training which wishes to change attitudes and behaviour, the message from research on group dynamics was fairly clear.

To summarise, then, small-group training methods have originated in the recognition of

● **the importance of assisting managers and supervisors to understand group processes, and to develop the interactive skills required to deal with people in groups and to work effectively in and with groups**

● **the small group as the most effective medium for bringing about attitude and behaviour changes**

The small group used for training purposes not only helps the manager to acquire new attitudes and to develop his interactive skills; it also allows him to observe group processes as they occur and thereby to improve his understanding of how groups work.

T-GROUPS

By far the best-known of the small-group approaches to training in interactive skills and social sensitivity is the T-GROUP. Although no longer describable as a recent development, it is still not widely used in Britain: to a majority of trainers it is probably more a thing they have heard about than one they have experienced. T-Groups are the prototype of small-group methods, and an examination of more recent developments cannot really be pursued without some prior consideration being given to the nature and aims of, and the objections to, T-Group Training.

So much has been written about T-Groups over the past few years that there is no need here to do more than pick out a few key points on what they are and what they try to do. Readers who are not very familiar with the literature will find a lot of useful information in two British publications, one a Training Information Paper by Peter Smith[4], the other a collection of papers from the Association of Teachers of Management, edited by Galvin Whitaker[5]. It may be helpful to mention, in passing, that the terms sensitivity training and laboratory training are often used synonomously with T-Group. However, these two terms are better regarded as generic ones, which include T-Groups, rather than as other words for the same thing.

T-Groups, and the laboratory approach to interactive skills training of which they are part, had their birth in the mid-1940s in the States. Those who were responsible for this innovation in applied group dynamics were in the main the people associated with the Research Centre for Group Dynamics. The term T-Group emerged in about 1949 in the training programmes offered by the newly-formed National Training Laboratory in Group Development, now known as the NTL Institute for Applied Behavioural Science.

A T-Group typically consists of six to ten individuals, most of whom will be strangers to one another, who meet together and with a trainer for a number of sessions over a period varying from a few days up to about two weeks. A key feature of the T-Group is that it has no specific agenda, no definite structure or organisation, and no agreed procedures. The task of the group initially is to fill the vacuum created by the lack of these familiar elements, and to study the way members behave as the group develops. The T-Group is often described as *unstructured* for obvious reasons. However, this is not a term its adherents like; they would say that it is structured in so far as it is committed to a method of learning by analysis of the member's own experiences in the group, and the objectives of learning are defined.

Another key feature is the role played by the trainer. His aim is to be as non-directive as possible, to avoid assuming or having thrust upon him the mantle of leader of the group. He will probably explain his role as being to assist the group to learn from examination of their behaviour; his interventions in the group will be rather infrequent, and when they do occur will most likely be to encourage members to focus on and own up to their own feelings about what is going on in the group, rather than to make judgments about others. As the group develops, the trainer will also help members to analyse and interpret what is happening. The essence of the T-Group, then, is that it provides a forum for the study of here-and-now behaviours, and also

**22 a critical survey
of training in
interactive skills**

a safe environment in which members can experiment with
new behaviours and learn about their consequences for
other members and for group functioning. The early stages
of the group's life are usually characterised by relatively high
degrees of uncertainty, suspicion, anxiety and tension. As
it develops, members begin to expose feelings and beliefs,
to give and receive feedback about their effects on each other,
and gradually to build up a climate of trust and ways of
dealing with the interpersonal and intragroup problems
with which they are confronted. It will be clear why the
label laboratory has become attached to this kind of learning
situation; the material of the situation is the behaviour of the
trainees themselves, the emphasis is on experimentation and
analysis, and the approach to learning is primarily an
inductive one.

**Expressions of the goals
of T-Groups are almost
as numerous as the
writers on the subject**

Expressions of the goals of T-Groups are almost as numerous
as the writers on the subject. In the briefest possible terms,
T-Groups aim, through intensive group self-study procedures,
to bring about increased sensitivity and skill in relation to
social-psychological phenomena occurring in interpersonal,
group and organisational situations. The NTL includes
amongst the goals for T-Groups
● the development of reality-centred leadership, defined
as leadership which helps the group in which it functions
to face and deal with all the relevant realities, including
personal and social ones, involved in solving the problems
they seek to solve
● the development in leaders of understanding and
sensitivity to group processes and skill in participating
effectively as leaders and members in these processes
Chris Argyris[6], in a paper which is now a classic, stresses
the purpose of changing members' values. The T-Group
provides an experience in which the ineffectiveness and
incompleteness of old values are revealed, and in which
new values come to be adopted as the group develops. He
goes on to say

*Basically it (the T-Group) is a group experience designed
to provide maximum possible opportunity for the individuals
to expose their behaviour, give and receive feedback,
experiment with new behaviour, and develop everlasting*

> *awareness and acceptance of self and others. The T-Group,*
> *when effective, also provides individuals with the opportunity*
> *to learn the nature of effective group functioning. They are*
> *able to learn how to develop a group that achieves specific*
> *goals with minimum possible human cost. . . . It is in the*
> *T-Group that one learns how to diagnose his own*
> *behaviour, to develop effective leadership behaviour and*
> *norms for decision-making that truly protect the wild-duck!*

Another emphasis to be found in statements of the aims of the T-Group is on members learning how to learn from their own interpersonal experiences, on the inculcation of an attitude of inquiry and experimentation. This is achieved through the learning of skills of observation, analysis and diagnosis of interpersonal situations.

The statement by Smith[4] of the goals of the T-Group succinctly sums up what most other writers have to say in their different ways. He gives three main goals

● increases in *sensitivity* – the ability to perceive accurately how others are reacting to one's own behaviour
● increases in *diagnostic ability* – the ability to perceive accurately the state of relationships between others
● increases in *action skill* – the ability to carry out skilfully the behaviour required by the situation. Action skill implies the ability to carry out a range of different behaviours and thus requires flexibility in choosing the right behaviour from a range of possible behaviours

These goals are notable for the fact that they are person-centred, making no reference to group processes as such, or to group development. Also, they do not refer directly to the change of values and attitudes as a goal. The latter omission is perhaps of significance in relation to what was said earlier about focusing on behaviour, rather than attitude, change in interactive skills training.

To what extent do T-Groups achieve the objectives that have been stated for them? One problem that we immediately come up against in looking for an answer to the question is that no widely accepted measures are available of the kinds of things that T-Groups are supposed to improve. Part of the fault here is that T-Group trainers have not described their objectives in behavioural terms, which might have allowed

T-Group trainers have not described their objectives in behavioural terms

**24 a critical survey
of training in
interactive skills**

changes to be observed and plotted. The studies that have been made of changes that occur during the training have mostly used self-report measures, such as questionnaires. These have shown that trainees do improve in sensitivity to interpersonal phenomena, and in self-awareness. Precisely what trainees do, or don't do, as a result of the training has not, however, been satisfactorily elucidated.

One other problem that makes it difficult to evaluate the effects of T-Groups is that the T-Group is usually just one of the methods used in laboratory training. Admittedly it is often the main method, but other more conventional techniques such as lectures, role-playing, and structured group discussions may be used in conjunction with it. The contribution of the T-Group *per se* to any changes that are identified either during training or in subsequent follow-up is therefore difficult to establish.

The real crunch question, of course, is whether the learning which undoubtedly takes place during the T-Group has any effect on job performance. The evidence here, such as it is, is ambiguous at best and inadequate at worst. Measures of job performance at management and supervisory levels are always difficult to obtain, and this has not helped follow-up research. Very few studies have been carried out, and the small number that meet the criteria of sound research design have relied on ratings and reports by colleagues of the trainees. Smith[4] after reviewing these studies concludes that *they provide good encouragement for the belief that T-Group training has a durable and beneficial outcome for substantial numbers of trainees.* However, some trainees apparently reveal no changes in job behaviour, and at least a few show negative or harmful changes.

Robert J House[7] reaches much the same conclusions as Smith in a careful review of the research literature on T-Groups. He cites six studies which utilised control groups, and concludes

> *All six studies revealed what appear to be important positive effects of T-Group training. Two of the studies report negative effects as well . . . all of the evidence is based on observations of the behaviour of the participants in the actual job situations. No reliance is placed on participant response;*

rather, evidence is collected from those having frequent
contact with the participant in his normal work activities.
Campbell and Dunnette[8] have also reviewed the evidence
on the impact of T-Group training. Their conclusions are
less optimistic than those of Smith and House. While
conceding that research shows that T-Groups produce
changes in behaviour, they point out that the usefulness of
the training in terms of job performance has yet to be
demonstrated. In a summary comment, they say
> . . . *the assumption that T-Group training has positive*
> *utility for organisations must necessarily rest on shaky ground.*
> *It has been neither confirmed nor disconfirmed. The authors*
> *wish to emphasise . . . that utility for the organisation is not*
> *necessarily the same as utility for the individual.**

One key reason why T-Group training apparently has little
or no effect on job performance is that participants often
return to a job environment which is in conflict with the
values and behaviours they have acquired during training.
What they have learnt might be described as the ability
to work more effectively in groups where the other members
have developed comparable skills and ways of looking at
and describing things. In other words, we are saying that the
learning may be specific to the group in which it has occurred.
Argyle[1] makes a similar comment:
> . . . *the situation is very oddly designed from the point of*
> *view of learning social skills, since the group is engaged on*
> *the very peculiar task of studying itself. There is no reason*
> *to expect that the social techniques which are successful here*
> *should work in other group situations – they would work only*
> *in other T-Groups.*

T-Groups are without doubt a controversial method of
interactive skills training. The feature for which they have
been most strongly attacked is their deliberate use of what
we might euphemistically call uncomfortableness, and the
tendency for their members to concentrate on their feelings
for and against each other. This can cause serious trouble
for more sensitive participants. Readers are referred to an
article by George S Odiorne[9] for an insight into the excessive
indignation that T-Group training can arouse.

* This problem is examined closely in chapter 3.

**26 a critical survey
of training in
interactive skills**

There are several other points about T-Groups which raise
reasonable doubts about them as a training method. The
most important one has already been mentioned, namely
the lack of an adequate specification of the behaviour
changes that will be brought about by the training. This
does not help the control of the training process. Control is
an important issue in its own right: to some extent the
group and its trainer seem to be at the mercy of the spon-
taneous behaviours that it generates. These may or may not
be conducive to appropriate learning. Feedback to trainees
is normally one of the primary control mechanisms in
learning; in T-Groups, as we have seen, much of the feedback comes from the members themselves. Such feedback
must inevitably be subjective, and it may suffer from
irrelevance. Finally, the role of the trainer, while it may be
non-directive, is certainly a very influential one for both
individual learning and group development. It is also
difficult, which means that few trainers can handle it
satisfactorily, and it is still but poorly understood.

We have dealt at such length with the nature and aims of
T-Group training because all other small-group methods
have affinities with the T-Group – particularly its aims. We
have also spent time on the doubts roused by the method
because subsequent developments in interactive skills
training have been motivated by the desire to overcome the
perceived weaknesses of the T-Group. The particular
developments we shall examine in the remainder of this
chapter have attempted to do one or more of four things.
Either they have attempted to structure the training group
more, for example by giving it specific tasks to accomplish,
thus drawing off some of the more emotive facets of group
behaviour. Or they have attempted to make feedback more
systematic and objective. Or they have attempted to integrate the training with on-the-job and organisational needs.
Or, finally, they have attempted to simplify, or even remove
altogether, the role of the trainer.

INSTRUMENTED LABORATORY TRAINING

The first development we shall mention is one that does not
have wide currency in Britain. It is usually known as
INSTRUMENTED LABORATORY TRAINING – we will use the

initials IT for short. It appears that the credit for originating
it should go to the well-known team of Robert R Blake
and Jane S Mouton. It grew out of a marriage between
research and conventional T-Group training, and seems to
have been used first in fully-fledged form in a Human
Relations Training Laboratory in about 1959.

What are the identifying characteristics of IT? How does it
differ from T-Group training? The most obvious difference,
and the one which gives the method its name, is the attempt
to make the feedback process more systematic, objective,
and relevant to the learnings that the method aims to bring
about. This is achieved through the use by the group of a
set of instruments – scales and measures – which are completed by members after each group session so that the
characteristics of group and personal action during each
meeting can be plotted on a wall-chart. The second difference follows from this, and it is that the trainer is removed
as a participant in the group. Whereas in the T-Group there
is a requirement for the trainer amongst other things to aid
feedback by calling attention to critical events occurring
within the group, and to create the conditions and provide
the model for members to become participant-observers of
group action, in IT it is the instruments that structure and
control the feedback process.

Instruments of other kinds, for example films and group
tasks, may be used in IT to initiate group activity. However,
like the T-Group, IT also makes use of the ambiguous,
unstructured group situation as a means of unfreezing
members' characteristic ways of behaving.

Another difference between T-Groups and IT that has been
identified is the relatively greater emphasis in the latter on
cognitive labelling and conceptual input, in contrast to the
stress on experiential learning in the former. The emphasis is
facilitated by the appropriate choice of feedback instruments.
Blake and Mouton[10] have described the three main types
of feedback instruments which they have developed for IT.
The first is the use of rating scales to identify variables
of group effort and interpersonal relationships in any
particular session. As the result of a good deal of research,
three group dimensions have emerged for measurement –

**28 a critical survey
of training in
interactive skills**

cohesion, group accomplishment and group development. Examples of specific scales that are used are *Group structure*, mechanistic-organic; *mutual support and trust among members*, respect and trust – disrespect and suspicion; *levelling*, completely closed and hidden concerning feelings and emotions – completely open; *group accomplishments*, fat and happy: completely coasting – lean and hungry: completely digging; *group development*, completely adequate – completely inadequate; *group cohesion*, best possible group – worst possible group.

The second type of feedback is provided by check lists. These are used to evaluate a variety of group and personal phenomena. Examples of phenomena for which lists have been devised are decision-making procedures, group climate, types of agenda items considered.

The third type uses rankings, which have been found useful for comparing members within a group on some aspect of personal behaviour. The rankings employed most frequently are of influence in the group.

The measures are completed by each member after each group session. The data are analysed by members, and summaries or averages for the group are plotted on wall-charts.

In Blake and Mouton's[10] view the goals of learning in IT and the T-Group are the same. That is, the primary aim is to aid participants in becoming more effective members of groups. Both are concerned with sensitivity training and skill training at the individual and group levels. However, Jay Hall[11] points out that trainers who favour the less structured T-Group approach feel that instrumentation is artificial if not antithetical to the goals of laboratory training. Hall suggests that the goals of the two approaches may not be identical, and from his own experience of both concludes that IT has clear **teaching** goals as compared with T-Groups, which emphasise personal learning processes. The advantages claimed for IT over the conventional trainer directed T-Group have been related to the key differences between them – ie the methods of feedback, and the presence/absence of the trainer as a group member.

Blake and Mouton[10] suggest the following advantages which

accrue from the use of instrumented feedback
▼ the feedback data emphasise the significance of feedback
and identify variables likely to be important for learning
▼ The quantitative aspect of the data assists participants
to see that it is possible to apply measures to interaction
processes, and that feelings are facts to consider and
understand
▼ participants can plot their own values against the group
average, a checking device through which members are
able to learn more about themselves relative to others as
standards
▼ longitudinal assessment of group development is possible
from session-to-session comparison of data, and a perspective
on change is maintained
▼ by plotting results for several groups on the same chart,
learning through intergroup comparison is facilitated
▼ the control of the scales helps to focus members'
attention on significant training dimensions
▼ results from the measures can be employed as
guidelines for placing training interventions into the overall
laboratory design to give emphasis, at designated intervals,
to certain features of group action
▼ the data provide a rich quantitative basis for research
on experiences of participants within the development
group
▼ the action research model, in which feedback of this sort
is central, can be used by participants in group learning
situations outside the laboratory; by their being an active
and integral part of the analysing, gathering and
interpreting of data, it appears that participants tend to
make more frequent and effective use of data outside the
laboratory
The last three of these claimed advantages should be
especially noted; if they are true, they mark really significant
steps forward.
They suggest that the main advantages of not having the
trainer participate in the development group are that
▼ the integrity of the group is not violated
▼ issues of dependency, counter-dependency, violated
expectations about leadership, trust of experts, and so on,

**30 a critical survey
of training in
interactive skills**

which tend to arise willy-nilly in the T-Group even though
not germane to the goals of training, are avoided
▼ many problems of control and organisation emerge
which seem to be more or less masked or eliminated when
a trainer is present in the situation
▼ the group is challenged and confronted with the
problem of discovering for itself, by whatever means it
wishes to use, ways of regulating its activities and directing
its movements and actions
▼ groups seem to learn how to experiment much more
quickly and effectively than do trainer-directed groups
Hall[11], in his discussion of the use of instruments in laboratory
training claims three other advantages for IT. All of them are
well worth noting. First, he says that not only does IT achieve
the goals sought by other approaches, but also it achieves
some unique effects. In particular, the identification of
concepts to the extent that learners can think about and
discuss their relevance and back-home implications is a
unique product of IT. Also, the design capability inherent
in the IT approach gives it more task relevance than many
approaches. The second important claim he makes is that
one need not be an expert to use instrumentation effectively.
Indeed, since instruments tend to be self-contained and
designed to focus attention on specific issues, learners themselves may use the instruments back home, thereby sharing
their learnings with their colleagues and speeding up the
transfer of knowledge to the organisation. Finally, he points
out that IT makes less demand on staff resources, since one or
two trainers can effectively handle large groups of learners
under the instrumented approach.
A great many of the advantages claimed for IT over the
T-Group have only speculative status, being deduced from
the differences between the approaches. Research is necessary
to establish their validity. Also, if evidence for the effectiveness of T-Groups is scanty, that for IT is even more so. This
makes it impossible to draw any firm conclusions about it.
Nevertheless, the quantitative approach to obtaining data
about group development which can be used for feedback,
and for establishing a measure of control over learning via
design, may be regarded as very significant developments.

If one criticism may be advanced it is that the data collection is limited to the trainees themselves, and covers only their perceptions of group events and development. What is missing still are data on the behaviours of group members and how these change over time. We have no knowledge of the objectives of the training in behavioural terms, nor of the extent to which the objectives are achieved.

THE MANAGERIAL GRID

The next major development of which we must take note is another one on which much has been written, and which many readers will know something about. It is again of American origin, and indeed has the same parentage as IT. It is the BLAKE MANAGERIAL GRID, otherwise known as Blake lab training, or simply grid training. A useful summary of the approach is provided in a paper by Blake, Mouton, Barnes and Greiner[12]. **This development in interactive skills training introduces several radical changes from the basic T-Group approach.** The two that will concern us here – a third is referred to later in this chapter – are: first, that **the training groups are much more task-oriented,** being provided with specific problems to solve or cases to discuss; second, **the learners are given a conceptual framework within which they can examine their own and fellow-members' styles of behaviour,** namely the Managerial Grid itself.

Managerial Grid training (abbreviated to MG) is on the fringes of interactive skills training as we have considered it up to now. The reason for this statement will become clearer as we proceed. Before describing the nature of the training, it is necessary to consider the general orientation which Blake and his colleagues adopt. MG training has its origins in a concern to improve organisational effectiveness as measured by productivity and profits. The task of the individual manager is to achieve production through people, a viewpoint with which this chapter began. In achieving this task, the manager has a concern both for productivity and for people: different managers show varying balances of these concerns. Blake suggests that managers can be characterised by their location on a two-dimensional grid – the Managerial Grid – one axis of which is labelled **concern**

for production and the other **concern for people.** Each axis, in Blake's representation of this idea, is a scale with nine points and so the location of a manager on the grid can be specified by two co-ordinates. It is at this stage in the exposition of the idea that a diagram is normally introduced. However, we will dispense with the visual aids, and simply say that Blake recognises, for illustrative purposes, five principal managerial styles

1,1 IMPOVERISHED MANAGEMENT; exertion of minimum effort to get done the work required to maintain organisation membership. Task effectiveness is unobtainable because people are indolent, passive and apathetic. Satisfactory human relations are difficult to achieve; but then, human nature being what it is, conflict is to be expected.

9,1 TASK MANAGEMENT; where a person is high in task efficiency but low in human satisfaction. In this approach, men are regarded as just another commodity – another instrument of production. Productive efficiency is achieved by arranging the conditions of work so that human interference is minimised. The executive's job is to plan, direct and control his subordinates' work.

1,9 COUNTRY CLUB MANAGEMENT; high human satisfaction but low work tempo. Getting the work out is incidental to elimination of conflict and the establishment of good fellowship. Being nice and considerate leads to the establishment of a comfortable home-from-home atmosphere which allows and requires an easy-going work tempo.

5,5 MIDDLE OF THE ROAD MANAGEMENT; adequate task performance while maintaining morale at a satisfactory level. A certain amount of production push, but don't go flat out. Be fair, be firm. Barely adequate performance is achieved while keeping morale at a satisfactory level.

9,9 TEAM MANAGEMENT; high task achievement from committed people who have a common stake in the firm's purposes, with good relationships of trust and respect. Production is achieved by the integration of task and human requirements into a unified system.

The MG may appear gimmicky; however, its theoretical foundations are sound, being based on the findings of a number of research studies, of which those of Fleishman[13] are perhaps the best known. MG training recognises the importance of the appropriate management style to the commitment, effort and satisfaction of individuals and work groups. The aim is to shift behaviour towards the (9,9) style, and the grid is useful as a framework within which behaviour can be examined, described and analysed. It also provides a common language for discussing behaviour.

In the MG seminar, which normally lasts a week, a modified T-Group approach is used to teach each participant how the other group members see his managerial style. Trainees are first familiarised with the grid language and theory, usually by pre-course work. The group then proceeds to work through a series of exercises and case problems, which allow each individual to exhibit his management style: this behaviour then becomes the object of feedback. Participants supposedly develop skills which enable them accurately and candidly to reflect the management behaviour of each individual. This process is intended to instil an appreciation for the human problems of production and move the trainees towards the (9,9) region of the grid.

The exercises on which groups work are designed to enable participants to achieve a better understanding of grid theories. Groups work under conditions of stress, fatigue and competition on the seminar; conflict arises fairly readily, and how individuals and groups learn to cope with it and obtain consistently high commitment to the tasks that have to be done is a central feature of the training. Group solutions to the exercises set are scored and recorded on charts. Participants' individual solutions can be compared with the group solution, and one group compared with another.

There is evidence that participants on MG seminars achieve a more accurate perception of their own style of behaving, which is tantamount to saying that their standards are raised. Blake has found, for example, that whereas before the seminar between 75 and 80 per cent of participants assess themselves as (9,9) managers, during the seminar the figure drops to between 25 and 30 per cent.

**34 a critical survey
of training in
interactive skills**

It is unfair to venture judgments on the effectiveness of MG seminars in producing improved job performance. Blake would not necessarily claim that they should, since the seminars themselves are only the first phase of a total training package. More of this later. We have concentrated on the seminar because it is most akin to the development that we have so far discussed, in that it does have individual learning as an objective, aims to bring about increased awareness of own behaviour and its impact on others, presumably seeks to change attitudes and behaviour, and relies on the small group as the medium for learning.

The significant features of MG training as a development from the other methods of interactive skills training we have examined are

● the introduction of a concern with production as well as interpersonal relationships
● the introduction of far more structure into the training via exercises, and a conceptual framework
● a shift away from group process as the primary source of learnings, towards a greater concern with task achievement

The use of quantified feedback on group task achievement, as a basis for comparing the effectiveness of different groups, and also the achievements of individual members, is worth noting. There is a carry-over here from the IT approach, although the types of measures in the two approaches are quite different.

One of the main reasons why we suggested that MG training is on the fringes of interactive skills training is that its concern is with gross behavioural style rather than with more specific skills. We noted very early in our discussion the origin of the MG approach in a concern with organisational effectiveness. The latter is a function of what behavioural scientists term organisational climate, which in turn is influenced by the general style of management exercised in the organisation. How one actually behaves in specific situations involving other people is a slightly different matter from the general style one tries to exercise. It seems that MG training may not be of any great assistance to the individual in this direction. We come back to the point that effective interactive skills training must assist individuals to distinguish what are the more appropriate behaviours in a given interactive situation and to practice these behaviours under conditions which provide them with feedback on their success. Of MG training we must ask, *what specific behaviours do participants develop? To what on-the-job situations are they relevant?* The answer might be that the training is more concerned with the macro than the micro aspects of behaviour, and that it is concerned to develop in participants a general orientation towards human relations problems rather than a set of specific skills.

COVERDALE TRAINING

The interactive skills training methods we have considered so far have originated in America. With the exception of one other development still to be discussed they probably represent the main lines of approach in use today in the States to improve peoples' facility in dealing with others in the work situation. T-Group training and MG training have also made an impact on the British side of the water, although they are certainly not rampant. The British manager's suspicion of anything new, especially if it comes from the other side, has held them in check, and perhaps rightly so. Now, however, we turn to a home-grown product, a development in interactive skills training known as COVERDALE TRAINING, after one of its main originators, Ralph Coverdale. Little has been written about this method, although a few years ago it received some publicity in connection with its application in Esso Petroleum, at Fawley Refinery in particular. The main sources of information for interested readers are a booklet produced by Training Partnerships[14] and a paper by Seamus Roche[15].

Coverdale Training does not own to any particular theoretical bias, although it clearly has roots, as do other small group methods, in general group dynamics theory. Its principal aims are to help managers to learn from experience, and to practice the skills of working with people. A T-Group adherent could not take exception to these; however, they are probably the only point of common ground between the approaches.

Coverdale Training groups are very definitely structured,

**36 a critical survey
of training in
interactive skills**

and the learning goals are fairly clearly defined. Unlike some other methods, the goals seem to lend themselves to measurement, although measuring instruments are not a feature of the method. What then is Coverdale Training? In the words of Training Partnerships

> *Coverdale Training is not a matter of teaching anybody anything. It is a system of planned experience, by which a man may begin to discover for himself certain lessons – and then go on learning from his subsequent experience.*

One might quibble over this definition: my own impression is that the method does have teaching goals as well as learning ones, and therein lie the seeds of some of its success. Coverdale Training has four main characteristics or principles

▼ managers learn by doing – practising the skills they need to get things done

▼ the training is centred around practical tasks – tasks which are actually performed rather than just talked about. The tasks are simply a vehicle to enable managers to learn skills of teamwork

(The tasks are the first element of structure in the training)

▼ managers learn a **systematic approach** to getting things done. The approach consists of the steps of doing something, analysing how it affects the situation, deciding what next requires to be done, planning how to do it, carrying the plan into action and repeating the sequence to improve performance. It provides the model for learning how to learn

(This is the second element of structure in the training. Here we have another framework that is offered to trainees; however it is a framework for doing, whereas that offered by MG training might better be described as one for reviewing. Both are aids to learning, and quite obviously are also teaching goals)

▼ learning takes place in groups. Each group develops its own social processes and personal interactions, which its members can study and, from this, learn. The group also provides a medium for its members to experiment with new ways of working together

The distinctive features, then, are the elements which give

structure to the training/learning situation – the tasks and the systematic approach. The basic Coverdale Training course lasts one week, and may be followed up by a second course six months to a year later. On the courses participants work through a series of tasks. The view is that the nature of the tasks is immaterial; they are, as noted earlier, a means of stimulating action, and a vehicle for learning. They are short, apparently straightforward and repeatable. Typical ones might be making as many four-letter words from Scrabble letters as possible in a given time; sorting playing cards; building a tower with Lego bricks; and so on. After carrying out a task, the group examines how they worked together and plan for better team performance on the next run. Although there is no deliberate emphasis on inter-personal phenomena, members quickly come to learn that people problems and group process problems interfere with getting the task done, and have to be planned to be overcome. The idea is that participants will learn to identify the particular strengths of members, and to integrate these into the team effort. Other points about the tasks are that it is believed the human and emotional issues which arise when people do things together are different from those which arise when people merely talk about what they might do in hypothetical circumstances; also, working at practical tasks, it is felt, provides a safety valve for tensions and frustrations. The systematic approach, which is perhaps the key learning/teaching goal, not only provides a model for learning. It enables members to work together and gives them a framework, against which they can assess the contributions of others and within which they can frame their own contributions. With its emphasis on processing problems to action, it helps members to bridge the gap between ideas and action. Finally, it is claimed that the systematic approach encourages members to deal more confidently with the issues of human interactions and emotions.

Coverdale Training is a good example of the reaction against the T-Group Coverdale Training is a good example of the reaction against the T-Group with its lack of structure, and of explicit behavioural goals, and with its focus on feelings, values and interpersonal problems. There is no mention of social sensitivity or of self-awareness although Training Partner-

D

ships say that surveys of managers who have been trained by the method show that they learn skills of observation and listening, and how to perceive the unique talents and capabilities of others. One of the biggest attractions of Coverdale Training to managers might well be its fairly straightforward, down-to-earth approach. There is no foisting of highfalutin theories on to participants, but rather an approach to problem-solving of a commonsense kind.

A problem in assessing the effectiveness of Coverdale Training is one that we have encountered with most of the other methods we have discussed – the lack of published evaluation studies which meet the accepted criteria of sound research design. Comments of a largely speculative nature are therefore all that can be offered. One doubt that can be entertained is about the sorts of tasks that are used in the training. Although the arguments advanced for using simple, short-cycle tasks can be appreciated, they are a long way removed from the kinds of tasks that managers have to deal with in real life, and there is at least a case for suggesting that they may generate patterns of behaviour and process snags different from, maybe narrower than, those the manager normally encounters. The research on interactive skills training jointly sponsored by BOAC and the Air Transport and Travel Industry Training Board[16], which subsequent chapters in this book say more about, has shown that Coverdale-type tasks do have some important limitations for mediating learning.

Another doubt arises about the nature of the interactive skills that Coverdale Training develops. There seems a strong possibility that what managers primarily acquire from the learning is a way of tackling problems – the systematic approach – which, let us hasten to say, is a very good thing to learn. However, they develop this skill with a group, where everyone else is doing the same, and it may be that it does not leave them well-equipped to deal with interpersonal problems which arise in other groups to which they return, where the members have not been exposed to the systematic approach.

The avoidance of much theoretical input into Coverdale Training, and of conceptualisation of interactive processes,

Coverdale-type tasks do have some important limitations for mediating learning

may detract from the participants' abilities to generalise their learning to a wider range of group problems than they have encountered during the training. The lack of conceptual constructs combined with an adherence to the systematic approach might conceivably reduce, rather than enhance, behavioural flexibility in dealing with interactive situations. It is not uncommon for some people to use an approach or system, that they have learned or been given, in a relatively rigid way as a panacea. It might be argued that this could not possibly happen with the systematic approach because it encourages managers to learn from experience, and opens them up to the consideration of novel solutions. However, while managers may well become open to new ways of behaving in the initial stages of the training, the system they learn may close them again before the course is over.

One last development in interactive skills training must be touched on before we conclude this survey. It is important because it recognises the specific element in interactive skills. In other words, it accepts that what people learn in a group situation may be how to relate to and deal with people in that group, and it may not help them a lot when they get into other groups. This is probably overstating things. However, there is little doubt that the relative lack of demonstrated success of the methods we have so far considered in improving job performance is due to incongruity between the learnings of the individual who has been on a course, and the job environment to which he returns. The point is, that whatever the method of training, the trainee leaves it with certain new values, ideas and ways of behaving. If there is no sympathy for these back home, and he is given no support in practising them, his learning will be lost.

TEAM TRAINING

The conclusion that follows from these considerations has led to the development of what is generally known as TEAM TRAINING. Briefly, the notion is that if the group method of training is to be used to help people to work better in and with groups, then the group should be one that has a life outside the training situation. Such a group might be a manager and his subordinates – the family group – or it might be people from different parts of an organisation

**40 a critical survey
of training in
interactive skills**

who have to work together from time-to-time – the cousin group. Thus the training is taken to the organisation, and in particular to work groups that already have an existence. The aim then is to release the full potentialities of the group, to assist it to work more effectively and productively on the real tasks that confront it, principally by sorting out the interactive problems in that group, helping members to deal with the interpersonal problems that distract them from the task in hand. It is the family group that is the preferred target of Team Training, as Blake, Mouton and Blansfield[17], for example, make clear. In the view of these authors, the group should study the actual difficulties of communication, control and decision-making which are related to existing problems of the organisation and of its operation.

It should be clear that Team Training is not a method as such. The methods used to train the organisational team might be any of the methods we have previously discussed. Adherents of each of the methods have seen Team Training as a desirable step forward, the most obvious way of over-coming the re-entry problem. MG training in its full form is in fact oriented towards improving organisational effective-ness through team development. The part we described earlier is the first phase of a six phase programme, and is the only part devoted to individual development. Coverdale Training, too, seeks to go beyond the training of managers in stranger groups to team, and organisational development. The paper by Blake et al[17] referred to above discusses a method of Team Training that is essentially of a T-Group kind. There are those who feel that the T-Group method is particularly unsuitable for Team Training because of the way it encourages participants to bare their feelings. It may do more harm than good for subordinate Fred to tell boss Bill precisely what he feels about him, or vice versa. I have sympathy with this view. It would seem that methods such as MG and Coverdale which concentrate on job behaviours, and assist the group to evolve effective task procedures, are more appropriate to Team Training.

In terms of improving the way in which people work to-gether in groups within the organisation, Team Training has an inescapable logic about it. However it has not been widely used, possibly because of the reluctance of organisations to release all the members of a work team for training at the same time. There has been little opportunity therefore to evaluate whether it is as effective as one might intuitively expect it to be. One study by Blake, Mouton, Barnes and Greiner[12] of the impact of a full scale application of MG training, involving all 800 managers in a division of a large petroleum company, does claim very substantial benefits resulting from the method. For example, the development programme lasted for approximately one year, and during that time the firm experienced a considerable rise in profits and decrease in costs, which the investigators claim cannot be explained on the basis of changes in the prices of raw and finished products, reductions in the labour force, and so on. However, it is the view of Campbell et al[18] that the worth of these results is difficult to judge. They make the very good point, which does emphasise the difficulties that face evaluators in this field:

> *A development programme that relies so heavily on group participation and team spirit must also live in the shadow of the Hawthorne effect. The specific content of the grid programme may have made little difference, but it is impossible to tell.*

We have now concluded our survey of what seem to be the main approaches current in America and this country to assisting people to deal more effectively with each other in the variety of interactive situations that occur at work. It is not the intention of this chapter to finish with a *Which*-like statement on the best buy. Enough has been said in discussing the methods to indicate that conclusions about their worth would be premature. Such research that has been done on the methods, and it is precious little, suggests that they do have an effect on the interactive skills of some people in certain situations. The fact that a conclusion has to be expressed in such vague terms really shows how inadequate our knowledge is about the precise nature of the effects of the interactive skills training that exists.

One of the biggest problems that developers of training are currently faced with is the lack of detailed descriptive data on interactive skills

One of the biggest problems that developers of training are currently faced with is the lack of detailed descriptive data on interactive skills. Early in this chapter, it was noted that

42 a critical survey
   of training in
   interactive skills

interactive skills have a behavioural component, and it was suggested that we might reasonably look for an explanation of why some individuals are better than others at dealing with people in terms of what they do. For most interactive situations – from which we can exclude the selection interview, on which quite a lot of work has been done – we cannot say specifically what the more skilful operator does that the less skilful doesn't or vice versa.

Part of the trouble, of course, is that it is very difficult to establish criteria of success in interactive situations: until this is done little progress can be made on separating effective behaviours from ineffective ones. These are fundamental deficiencies. Because of them, a range of other questions which is very important for designing training, just cannot be answered. **Are there identifiable patterns of behaviour which are consistently more successful in certain classes of interactions? Are specific behaviours of any significance at all, or is it that general style is the important thing? To what extent does improving a person's ability to deal with one kind of interactive situation generalise to other situations?** A particular case of the last question is relevant to the trend towards small group methods in training – **does training designed to assist a manager to function more effectively as leader or member of a group also improve his skill in dyad interactions?**

Against this background of substantial ignorance about interactive skills, it is obviously very difficult both to identify training needs, and to specify training objectives, in any but the broadest terms. We have raised questions in respect of all the training methods described above about what they actually achieve in the way of behaviour change. They claim, for example, that managers are helped to learn the skills of teamwork. But what does this mean in terms of the behaviours that an individual learns? How do we recognise that the manager has learnt the skill, and how do we determine his progress in learning? **What can the manager do, or what is he willing to do – in actions that can be observed – at the end of training that he was unable or unwilling to do before?**

The failure to answer such questions satisfactorily must constitute our main criticism of the approaches to interactive skills training developed to date. We do not know what the training achieves in the way of observable and measurable behaviour change. It is a serious criticism, because if the effects of training are not measured, then it is very difficult to maintain control over the teaching/learning process. This is a situation that would not be tolerated in other kinds of training. Continuous monitoring of the trainee's performance is accepted as a condition of learning; it is the source of feedback, and also the basis for modifying the learning situation to make it more relevant to the trainee's rate and stage of progress.

If the earlier parts of the chapter have been digested, it may be objected that the IT method in particular uses measures which can assist the control of training, and therefore is immune to the above criticism. This is partly true. But, the measures are subjective ratings or rankings provided by the trainees, and in the main they measure the development of the training **group.** This is fine if the objective of the training is to produce an effective group – as in fact Team Training aims to do. However, since most interactive skills training takes place with stranger groups, its objective must be to develop individual skills, not group skills. Neither IT, nor any of the other methods, systematically use measures of individual behavioural change.

One last criticism of the approaches we have described. It is one we have already implied, namely that the approaches are blanket ones which treat all-comers as having the same entry levels of skill, and for whom the learning experiences are equally relevant at all stages of the training. Practitioners of the approaches may deny that they make any such assumptions: what is important is that whether they do or not, they cannot **do** much about it – because they do not identify initial skill levels, nor monitor changes in skills on an individual basis as the training proceeds.

The implications of these criticisms should be clear. A vital requirement in the further development of interactive skills training is for behavioural measures that can be applied to individuals to diagnose their strengths and needs on entry,

**44 a critical survey
of training in
interactive skills**

and to control the training/learning process in such a way
that learning experiences can be designed to give each
trainee at all times the best possible chance of profiting from
them. A tall order? Perhaps. But over the last two years
work has been going on in Britain which holds the bright
promise of meeting the requirement. It has now reached the
stage where the people and organisations involved believe
that sufficiently encouraging findings have been accumulated
from the research and development effort for progress to be
publicised.

Two things only remain to be said. The first is that all of us
who have been associated with this development in interactive skills training are excited by the achievements so far.
It is felt that a really significant step forward has been made.
The second is that we still have a long way to go.

bibliography

[1] **ARGYLE, M.** The Psychology of Interpersonal Behaviour.
London. Penguin Books. 1967.

[2] **MAIER, N R F** and **ZERFOSS, L R.** MRP: A Technique for
Training Large Groups of Supervisors and its Potential Use in
Social Research. *Journal of Human Relations*, 5, 1952. pp 177-186.

[3] **SOLEM, A R.** Human Relations Training: Comparison of
Case Study and Role Playing. *Personnel Administration*, 23, 1960.
pp 29-37.

[4] **SMITH, P B.** Improving Skills in Working with People: the
T-Group. *Training Information Paper 4.* 1969. London. HMSO.

[5] **WHITAKER, G.** T-Group Training: Group Dynamics in
Management Education. *ATM Occasional Papers 2.* 1965. Oxford.
Basil Blackwell.

[6] **ARGYRIS, C.** T-Groups for Organisational Effectiveness.
Harvard Business Review, 42 (2). 1964. pp 60-74.

[7] **HOUSE, R J.** T-Group Education and Leadership Effectiveness:
A Review of the Empirical Literature and a Critical Evaluation.
Personnel Psychology, 20, 1967. pp 1-32.

[8] **CAMPBELL, J P** and **DUNNETTE, M D.** Effectiveness of
T-Group Experiences in Managerial Training and Development.
Psychological Bulletin, 70, 1968. pp 73-104.

[9] **ODIORNE, G S.** The Trouble with Sensivity Training.
Journal of the American Society for Training and Development,
17 (10), 1963. pp 9-20.

[10] **BLAKE, R R** *and* **MOUTON, J S.** The Instrumented Training Laboratory. *Issues in Training.* Ed. Weschler, I R and Schein, E H. 1962. Washington. National Training Laboratories.
[11] **HALL, J.** The Use of Instruments in Laboratory Training. *Journal of the American Society for Training and Development,* 24 (5). 1970. pp 48-55.
[12] **BLAKE, R R, MOUTON, J S, BARNES, J S** *and* **GREINER, L E.** Breakthrough in Organisation Development. *Harvard Business Review,* 42, 1964. pp 133-155.
[13] **FLEISHMAN, E A.** Leadership Climate, Human Relations Training and Supervisory Behaviour. *Personnel Psychology,* 6, 1953. pp 205-222.
[14] **COVERDALE TRAINING FOR DEVELOPMENT,** London. Training Partnerships. 1967.
[15] **ROCHE, S.** Coverdale Management Training. *Manpower and Applied Psychology,* 1 (1), 1967. pp 19-26.
[16] **RACKHAM, N.** Development and Evaluation of Supervisory Training. Research report 71/1. Staines: Air Transport and Travel ITB. 1971.
[17] **BLAKE, R R, MOUTON, J S** *and* **BLANSFIELD, M G.** How Executive Team Training Can Help You. *Journal of the American Society for Training and Development,* 16 (1), 1962. pp 3-11.
[18] **CAMPBELL, J P, DUNNETTE, M D, LAWLER, E E** *and* **WEICK, K E.** Managerial Behaviour, Performance and Effectiveness. New York. McGraw-Hill. 1970.

the search for
new methods in
INTERACTIVE SKILLS
training

NEIL RACKHAM

The attraction of hindsight is that it makes life simple. When events are seen in retrospect, the blind alley need never have been taken, mistakes can evaporate and the messy chaos of uncertainty can be transformed into an intricate network of purposeful events. Not that this transformation is undesirable. This chapter, for example, which is the first in a series describing the results of over ten man-years of training research and development, uses the hindsight of our research team to spare readers from a tedious catalogue of our errors and uncertainties. So we write about areas of success; for our failures and uncertainties are like everybody else's – depressing, time-consuming and unspeakably tedious to hear about second-hand.

BUT WRITING IN A WAY WHICH SELECTIVELY DESCRIBES those parts of our development which have been successful, has one danger. It gives a flatteringly positive impression of the work which we have done. The practising trainer may look through the chapters of this book and detect a depressing gap between the coherent world of each author, where success seems to come easily, and the messy realities of his own job, where time and opportunity are so limited. Now, evaluation studies have shown that carry-over of training to the job is especially low where there is a perceived disparity between the training ideal and the job reality. The same is true for these chapters. If trainers feel that our account is cut off from the uncertainty, difficulty and frequent failure of the trainer's real situation, then nothing we have written will be put into practice. And that would defeat our purpose in writing, which has been to encourage trainers to implement and put into everyday use, some of the new methods which have been developed in our work.

So it would seem appropriate to preface our ideas with an assurance that the situations in which we developed these new methods were no easier or more favourable than many other in-company environments – that although readers are saved from sharing our blind alleys, we inevitably wandered through a maze of them – that we were continually faced with the problems of inadequate time and resources, which prevented us from moving as quickly or as purposively as we would have liked. In short, the developments which we shall describe arose, in fairly normal large-company environments, as practical attempts to deal with training situations which were typically messy and difficult. And because we believe that our experience may be useful to others in a whole variety of training situations, we have written this book in the hope that readers will take, and adapt to their own use, some of the methods which we have developed. And to help them do this, the seventh of our chapters is a do-it-yourself guide, showing how an afternoon's work will enable any trainer to incorporate one or more of our methods into his existing training programmes, with measurable and beneficial results. So please plagiarise, copy, adapt, modify or develop anything which you read in these chapters.

48 the search for
new methods in
interactive skills
training

Finally, before we get down to the hard work of detailed explanations, don't discount these methods because of their titles or jargon. Interactive skills training sounds a specialised, even esoteric, training area. But we believe our methods will prove useful on a broader front to any trainer who, for example, has syndicate groups in his courses, or runs any form of group project work.

Now to the central issue, interactive skills training, which we define as any form of training which aims to increase the effectiveness of an individual's interaction with others. This is a broad definition, covering areas such as communications and human relations, as well as specific methods such as T Groups, Coverdale training or Blake's grid. Because there is no single, agreed, generic term for training in these areas, many other names exist, including organic skills, inter-personal skills, social skills and people skills. All these terms are broadly interchangeable, but for the sake of coherence, we adopt the term INTERACTIVE SKILLS to describe the whole field.

Like so many new developments, our work had its roots in dissatisfaction with existing methods

Like so many new developments, our work had its roots in dissatisfaction with existing methods. In 1968, BOAC, in common with many other companies, was trying to find a training technique which would improve people's interactive skills. The BOAC target population consisted primarily of supervisors, and there were no ready-made techniques which adequately catered for a supervisory population. So it was decided to develop an in company course, using the internal resources of BOAC General Training Department and employing whichever methods seemed most effective. After some initial experiments by Peter Honey and his colleagues, the form of training chosen was the task-centred group, where groups of six to eight supervisors worked together on a series of tasks, with the trainer making comments and guiding the group towards a better understanding of how individuals should interact. At the time, this was a common training method in the United States and was becoming popular in this country in several specific forms such as Coverdale training and Action Centred Leadership. Because BOAC was undertaking validation studies of its other training programmes, it seemed a logical development also to try to measure the effectiveness of the new task-centred training. So I was called in from the Sheffield University Training Evaluation Unit to work with Peter Honey on methods of measuring the training and its effects. We began, as a later chapter describes, by observing the behaviour of each group during training, using videotape and standard interaction analyses such as the Bales system. We soon made six awkward discoveries which, at the time, disturbed us considerably.

● We could measure changes in people's behaviour during the training, but these changes were unpredictable, relatively random and almost completely outside the trainers' control.

● The measuring instruments we were using, particularly the Bales analysis, were hopelessly inadequate. We had videotape recordings taken at each stage of the course and these revealed that certain important behaviour changes were taking place which the Bales analysis completely failed to detect.

● Guidance from the trainer in the form of interventions – even when that trainer was a psychologist – did not detectably influence the behaviour change of the groups. So that groups where the trainer said nothing at all showed as much change as groups where experienced and skilled trainers attempted to influence group progress by making observations and interventions.

● Changes in behaviour were almost entirely dependent on the group that an individual was in. If that particular mix of people suited him, then his behaviour changed; if he was incompatible in some respect, no changes took place. This made the training disturbingly luck-of-the-draw, being dependent on the chance factors by which people were put into their working groups.

● There was no correlation between actual behaviour change and each individual's perceptions of his behaviour. Consequently, at the end of the course, there were individual course members who felt that they had changed enormously, but had not done so according to any of our measures. Conversely, there were individuals who had changed significantly but who did not perceive any change in themselves. A typical, and disturbing, end of course comment was, *I think the training has done something for me, but I'm not sure what.*

● Course members perceived the training as highly enjoyable but having very little relevance to their jobs. One of the author's earlier research studies, also carried out in BOAC, had shown that when training sessions were rated low for relevance, then carry-over to the job was minimal. So it seemed likely that the job carry-over from task-centred training would be very low indeed.

So, with these six pieces of unpalatable evidence on their hands, Peter Honey and his colleagues were faced with a difficult choice. Should they accept these major inadequacies in the training, excusing themselves on the grounds that other forms of task-centred training were no better? Or should they invest enormous time and energy, committing the training department's pressed resources to the development of a new training system and new methods of measuring its effectiveness?

They decided to start again, questioning all of their assumptions, and attempting to build a system of interactive skills training which would meet the following criteria:

▼ It would be CONTROLLED, so that trainers could influence and predict the immediate outcome of the training with considerably greater accuracy than could be achieved by any existing form of interactive skills training.

▼ It would be MEASURED continuously, using specially devised behaviour analysis systems which would be more sensitive to changes in group performance than existing systems such as Bales.

▼ It would be FLEXIBLE, so that it could be modified to develop specific sets of behavioural skills, or to be appropriate for the needs of different levels in the organisation.

▼ It would be ORGANISATIONALLY RELEVANT, based on key organisational behaviours diagnosed from new, and sophisticated, forms of training needs analysis.

▼ It would be POWERFUL, so that significant changes in behaviour occurred in the majority of course members.

▼ It would be LOW-RISK, so that individual course members would be under minimal stress.

▼ It would be ECONOMICAL, so that it would need minimal skills and resources and would avoid obvious wastefulness such as course members who, because they happened to be in an unsuitable working group, made no progress.

Our extraordinarily demanding specification was for a form of interactive skills training which was controlled, measured, flexible, organisationally relevant, powerful, low-risk and economical

So, in a sentence, our extraordinarily demanding specification was for a form of interactive skills training which was controlled, measured, flexible, organisationally relevant, powerful, low-risk and economical. Small wonder that it has taken us over ten man-years of development to have achieved these objectives.

But let us return to 1968, where Peter Honey and his colleagues were meeting in BOAC with the gloomy task of trying to bridge an enormous gap between the ineffective type of interactive skills training which existed and the specification for an effective form which seemed an impossibly ambitious objective. The first thing which we decided was a matter of demarcation. Previous co-operation between the training staff and the researcher had shown that much more was done, and the results had greater practical payoff, when the traditional boundaries between training, research and evaluation were broken down. So we decided to do away with formal role boundaries. In the development which followed, most of the research data was collected by trainers, the researcher had an integral part in the training process and both researcher and trainers worked together on problems of design and development.

But before we could finally commit ourselves to intensive investigation and development, we first had to ask ourselves questions about priorities. **Should we really be putting our resources into improving people's interactive skills anyway? What made us think that this area had a greater priority than, for example, technical skills?** So we started by turning our attention to the analysis of training needs. It was at this stage that we came across a major stumbling block – the inadequacy of the classic job description approach to training needs analysis. At the time, the researcher was undertaking a study in the chemical industry which provided us with some concrete

**52 the search for
new methods in
interactive skills
training**

evidence of the extent of this inadequacy. Among a group
of supervisors, when technical and interactive skill needs
were compared, the relative proportion of training needs
arising from the job description approach was 80 per cent
technical and 20 per cent interactive. Consequently, it
would seem fair to conclude that technical skills constituted
a significantly greater training priority than interactive
skills. However, when a different form of training needs
analysis was used with the same group, this being the
CRITICAL INCIDENT TECHNIQUE, which asks people to describe
those incidents in any time period which gave them difficulty,
the proportion was almost reversed with 30 per cent technical
skills need and 70 per cent interactive skills need. Why this
disparity? And which system should be used to establish
training priorities?

We concluded that the job description approach focused
trainers' attention **inwards** towards the individual and
those things which went on within his job boundary. As a
result, technical skills appeared disproportionately important,
because interactive skills, by definition, went **outwards**
across the job boundary. So training needs analysis based
on job description did not give adequate information
about interactive skills needs, which always lay at the interface between jobs. What is more, there was increasing
evidence, from our own studies and elsewhere, that an
organisation's effectiveness was much more influenced by
effective interactions between jobs than by effectiveness
within each job boundary. So we ultimately came to the
following conclusion, which we would like other trainers to
consider because it greatly influences the relative priorities
of training.

**The primary limitation on supervisory, or managerial,
effectiveness lies, not within each job boundary, but
at the interface between jobs. This limitation, which
can be countered by interactive skills training, is not
revealed by the classic job description approach to
training needs analysis, so that many trainers underestimate its significance in their organisations.**

Having re-examined the need for interactive skills training,
and having clarified our ideas by producing the seven

criteria against which to judge any method, we decided to take another look at available methods elsewhere. We hoped either to find one which fulfilled most of our criteria or, quite frankly, to pinch and adapt any good ideas we could lay our hands on. As it turned out, good ideas were few and far between, and those few we found were not amenable to plagiarism. Certainly no existing method came near to meeting our criteria.

We felt most existing forms of interactive skills training to be seriously deficient in a number of ways. In particular, there were three major flaws which marred almost every method which we examined. As these flaws are just as common, and just as serious, as they were in 1968, it may be useful to examine them briefly.

The first, and most common, error we called the golden rule fallacy. In its purest form it existed in the old, largely discredited human relations training of the '40's and '50's. However, its influence is still clearly visible in most modern forms of interactive skills training. The golden rule fallacy suggests that there is a right way to interact, and that this right way is common to all men in all organisations. Social science research, and some of our own work in this area is described in the next chapter, has shown that this naïve assumption is complete nonsense. We have found that behaviour patterns which are seen as right in BOAC, for example, are very different from those seen as right in International Computers. And each reader's experience should confirm that the way in which we interact with others is, to a large extent, situationally dependent and cannot be reduced to a simple right-wrong set of golden rules.

Yet it is tempting to abandon reality, which is complex and messy, for the simple, clean fantasy of the golden rule. But needless to say, those who give way to this temptation – and we found many commercially-run training courses which did – are living in a dangerous cloud-cuckoo land. These golden rules are very like the alchemists' Philosopher's Stone. And just as the development of natural science has finally and inconveniently put an end to the attractive idea that a magic powder will turn everything to gold, so the social

**54 the search for
new methods in
interactive skills
training**

sciences during the last 30 years have forever discredited any attempts to find golden rules which will suddenly cause people to interact effectively. There are no such rules; there never will be. Yet credulous training managers are still taken in by the alchemists of interactive skills training who claim to have discovered the right way.

It seemed to us that those people who had invented golden rule training methods were generally naïve crusaders who had ideas about what should be and were trying to bend reality to fit their concepts. The lesson for us was that our starting point had to be a close examination of what really happened in interactive situations, rather than starting from a fixed idea of what should happen.

The second flaw in most existing types of interactive skills training was what we called goal obsession. In simple terms, going through goal-obsessed training was very like being given a map which had your destination marked on it in great detail. It was fine if you knew where your starting point was and which roads led to your destination. But if you didn't know where you were on the map to begin with, then details about your destination were largely wasted. The first, and most important, thing which any map reader needs to know is where he is now. Transferring this analogy back to interactive skills training, goal-obsessed training spends the majority of its effort describing and examining effectiveness in interactive terms – in other words, describing the destination or goal – and too little of its attention is paid to the crucial problem of what managers' existing behaviour patterns are – the starting point. The nearest form which we found was Blake's Grid*, which gave some starting point information based on a person's initial perception of his own behavioural style in terms of his position on the grid, subsequently supplemented by subjective perceptions of other course members. However, as we have already mentioned, such perceptions, in our situation at least, had proved highly unreliable, showing no correlation with actual behaviour patterns.

Consequently, we realised that any successful redesign of interactive skills training had to incorporate some mech-

see chapter 1

anism which permitted an accurate, objective and quantified account of each course member's existing behaviour patterns, if we were to avoid goal-obsession. Until we had some means of showing people where they actually were on our interactive map, we could scarcely be surprised if they seemed lost and unable to reach the training destination.

The third flaw, which seemed common to every form of interactive skills training which involved people working in groups, we called grouping accidents. In our own course designs we had found that the amount of behaviour change that people showed was primarily dependent on the group which they found themselves in. It therefore seemed little short of crazy for people to go on one of the various interactive skills training courses and find themselves, by chance, in a group which could easily negate the whole training experience for them. Yet none of the existing forms of training had developed an objective and reliable means of predicting which groupings would suit particular participants best and which would bring about most behaviour change. As a result, much of the potential effectiveness of existing methods was being lost.

We decided that this was a vitally important area for investigation, especially as it was likely to show a worthwhile pay-off in other training areas such as the problem of choosing effective syndicate or project groups in more conventional training situations. Consequently we put considerable effort into solving this problem and came up with some very successful results which are discussed in later chapters.

It would be wrong to conclude that we were critical of every aspect of existing interactive training methods. In particular, **there were two features of most methods which we had already incorporated into our initial task-centred training and intended to continue in any new development which we might make.**

We were convinced that any acceptable method needed to be completely open and to hide nothing from participants. With very few exceptions, existing forms of interactive skills training were exemplary in this respect, being entirely frank about their aims, methods, risks and processes. This openness seemed to us to be more

**56 the search for
new methods in
interactive skills
training**

necessary in the interactive skills field than in any other. A training process which alters a person's skills in a technical area, such as operating a machine or using matrix statistics, has a negligible potential for influencing his social life outside of the work situation. However, a training process which changes a person's interactive behaviour may have the most profound effects on every aspect of his life. If interactive skills training is to be ethically acceptable, it must be of the highest integrity – and openness towards the individual who goes through the training is a necessity. We had strong views about maintaining a high level of openness and integrity in the design and development of our courses, which led us to adopt the code of practice which is discussed in chapter 6.

The other feature of most existing methods, which we adopted because we felt it essential to any effective design of interactive skills training, was the method of training through groups. As Peter Honey has pointed out, a skill can be acquired only through practice: an interactive skill is no exception. We would not expect somebody to be able to swim solely as a result of attending lectures or of reading books about swimming. Like other skills, swimming depends on practice – in real or very closely simulated situations. Similarly, we should not expect a person to interact more effectively with others if we deny him ample training opportunity for practising new patterns of interaction, whether this be in two person groups or the more commonly used training groups containing six to eight people. Surprisingly enough, we found a number of forms of interactive skills training which did not allow a significant amount of interactive practice in the training design. These forms depended on traditional techniques such as lectures, films and individual exercises. We surmised that they would, at best, be no more effective than our hypothetical training programme which used lectures in an attempt to teach people how to swim.

But, as we found in 1968, it is always easier to criticise existing methods than to build up something better. And although it would be tempting to pretend in retrospect that we had a clear idea of the way forward, in fact we were uncertain and rather confused. However, **one guiding principle existed from our previous evaluation studies in other areas of BOAC. This was the cybernetic maxim that systematic improvement in performance can take place only through feedback. If there is no feedback, performance cannot systematically improve.** This set us thinking about how group members obtained feedback about their interactive skills. It seemed that there were two sources – the trainer, and other group members. Now, our earlier findings had cast some doubt on the effectiveness of the trainer as a means of feedback. And we knew that feedback from the complex, often contradictory, sources within the group was unlikely to be adequate for systematic performance improvement. So it appeared that one of the weakest points in our, or any other, form of group centred training was the lack of a controlled, objective system of feedback. The more we examined this conclusion, the more sense it made. It explained, for example, why T-Groups are so acceptable to social scientists, who are generally highly skilled in extracting feedback from complex group situations, and so much less acceptable to managers, who are normally less practised in this area. Moreover, it exposed a great weakness in most forms of interactive skills training. Almost by definition, the people most in need of interactive skills training are those who are least capable of extracting accurate feedback in interactive situations. Thus, with T-Groups for example, those who need them most are the ones least likely to benefit from them.

Consequently, it seemed that if our new method was to be effective it had to be based on a system for providing participants with accurate feedback on their performance. Which meant that we had to develop a reliable and valid means of measuring people's performance in order to produce this feedback.

Our first attempts started with videotape. We spent many tedious weeks running and re-running spool after spool of recordings which we had made of working groups during training. In particular we were looking for behaviours which showed change during our training programmes. We were less interested, at this stage, with those behaviours which

One of the weakest points was the lack of a controlled objective system of feedback

**58 the search for
new methods in
interactive skills
training**

appeared relatively static or resistant to change. At the end of our videotape exercise, we had produced a short-list of 27 behaviour types, or categories, which showed some degree of change in frequency during the task-centred interactive skills training courses which we had been running. We then tried out various combinations of these behaviours, developing a set of criteria which allowed us to reduce our initial 27 to a manageable dozen or so categories. This part of our work is described in greater detail in subsequent chapters, so that we can skim through it relatively quickly here. The series of behaviour categories which we developed showed high reliability between different users and were more intelligible to course members than the Bales categories which we had been using earlier. Moreover, both our new analysis instrument, and a number of variants on it, showed certain significant changes in individual and group performance which the Bales analysis had failed to detect.

BEHAVIOUR ANALYSIS

Our new instrument for measuring group performance, which we called a BEHAVIOUR ANALYSIS, directly met the second of our seven criteria for an effective system of interactive skills training – the criterion of measurement. It provided a means of continuously and reliably measuring changes in individual and group performance during training and gave us data which could be used for performance feedback to participants. It also provided us with data which allowed us to make running changes in the course design – such as changing the membership of working groups in order to increase the overall level of behaviour change. As a later chapter describes, this particular capacity to mix the composition of groups on the basis of behaviour analysis results has, in many instances, trebled or quadrupled the amount of individual behaviour change resulting from the training. This is not surprising because, as we have already discussed, behaviour change is largely group-dependent. Behaviour analysis data has allowed us to do away with the grouping accidents, where an arbitrarily composed group restricts individual behaviour change.

So far our design was relatively straightforward in theory, consisting of a carefully developed set of behaviour measures, continuously recorded by the trainer during group activities, and leading on the one hand to individual and group feedback and on the other to running design changes.

The practice was slightly more complex. Before any individual could receive useful feedback, even from a well constructed, scrupulously recorded behaviour analysis system, he had to be observed during interaction with a range of people, in a range of situations, so that a representative sample of his behaviour patterns could be recorded. In our experience, the average group member needed about two course days of continuous observation before we could give him a reliable picture of his own behaviour. To have offered him feedback before this would have been dangerously misleading. As a result, during the first two to three days of a course individuals worked in groups, usually of six to eight people, while their behaviour was recorded continuously using a behaviour analysis technique, by a trainer attached to the group. In that time, group members worked at a variety of tasks and situations, and received no feedback from the trainers about their interactive behaviour. This, the information-collecting phase of the training, we called the DIAGNOSTIC STAGE.

Once a reliable sample of people's behaviour had been collected, we could then enter the next stage. This consisted of processing the information from the behaviour analysis and other sources, putting it into a coherent form suitable for providing each individual with feedback on his existing behaviour patterns. And because this is at the very heart of our system, one of the chapters in this book deals exclusively with the techniques which we have since developed in the processing/feedback area, including computer-based feedback.

Following the formal feedback stage, the final part of the training was designed to be considerably more fluid than the earlier stages. The diagnostic stage, of course, needed to be relatively structured and controlled in terms of group activity and trainer observation, so that reliable behaviour samples could be obtained. In contrast, the final stage was one where individuals were free to practise and develop new behaviour patterns, with the trainer providing monitoring information from the behaviour analysis to give each individual specific feedback on his performance. Right from the start of our development, groups were given considerably more freedom in this stage of the training and encouraged to choose their own activities whenever possible.

FIGURE 1 outlines a typical structure for the design of our earlier courses.

1 typical interactive skills course design

	Diagnostic Stage	Formal Feedback	Practice + Monitoring Feedback Stage
GROUPS	Undertake wide range of activities, giving reliable behaviour samples.	Trainers give groups and individuals feedback on their interactive performance during the diagnostic phase.	Undertake further Activities to develop and practice new behaviour patterns. Receive feedback from trainers to gauge success of attempts at behaviour change.
TRAINERS	Record group behaviour using behaviour analysis, but giving no feedback to groups or individuals.		Record group behaviour using behaviour analysis, giving individuals feedback on their performance whenever appropriate.
	Days 1 to 3	Day 3	Day 3 plus

This basic outline persisted in our subsequent developments which other chapters in the book describe. However, as FIGURE 4 shows, even though our present procedure can be traced to the basic structure of FIGURE 1, our thinking since then has become considerably more sophisticated.

One of the practical difficulties of the simple design which we have just described is that it operates with only two classes of people – course members and trainers. As training grows more complex, so the trainer's role becomes more demanding. This can easily lead to a serious overload, as FIGURE 2 shows.

2 the trainer functions in interactive skills training

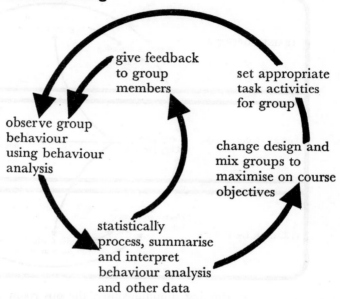

give feedback
to group
members

set appropriate
task activities
for group

observe group
behaviour
using behaviour
analysis

change design and
mix groups to
maximise on course
objectives

statistically
process, summarise
and interpret
behaviour analysis
and other data

The combined trainer functions illustrated in FIGURE 2 place an impossibly heavy load on an individual trainer. Even if an individual trainer was sufficiently energetic and able to undertake the arduous double role of observing and processing data, it would be unreasonable to expect him also to change and monitor such things as group composition. Because of this, we decided to hive off the data processing and design change functions, leaving the trainer with the more manageable functions of recording group behaviour and feeding back the interpreted data to his group. FIGURE 3 illustrates a more realistic distribution of the trainer functions. We handled all of the statistical functions in a central operations room. Completed behaviour analysis sheets, together with semantic differential measures of each group member's perceptions of the session, were brought to the ops room after every work session. With three groups

**62 the search for
new methods in
interactive skills
training**

3 splitting the trainer functions

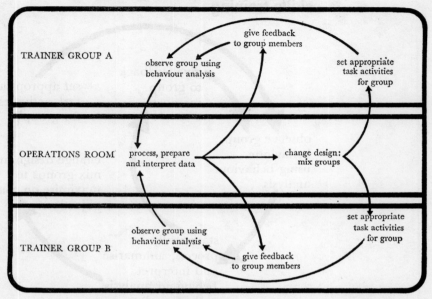

running simultaneously, the ops room was handling up to
50 000 items of information, from 700 or more pieces of
paper, during a five-day course. Before giving feedback to
group members, trainers met in the ops room and discussed
each individual's behaviour patterns with the ops room
staff, who had prepared a complete record of each individual's
behaviour to form the basis of feedback.

Peter Honey and I have produced the model in FIGURE 4
to show how trainer and ops room functions fitted in with
group activities, feedback and course design. Although the
model includes only twelve group activities, the actual
number on any course was likely to be about 30. As the
model shows, feedback became more intensive as the course
progressed, so that in the first monitored practice stage,
course members obtained feedback – if they wished it – at
the end of each working session, when the trainer showed
them the completed behaviour analysis sheet and discussed

the behavioural content of the session. In the second monitored practice stage the trainer would, if he felt it appropriate,
intervene at any point in his group's working session to give
feedback or to make any contribution which he considered
helpful. Although we distinguish these two stages in the
model, in practice one merged into the other, with trainers
taking an increasingly active role as the course progressed.

LONG-CYCLE FEEDBACK

So far we have only discussed one kind of feedback – the
behaviour analysis information given by the trainer to
course members. Another equally important type of feedback has also taken place, on a longer time cycle, using the
data from each course to modify the design of the next. In
this way we have developed a self-correcting training system
of the kind discussed by Warr, Bird & Rackham in the book
THE EVALUATION OF MANAGEMENT TRAINING. We have been
able systematically to alter the design, in terms of such
variables as group size, types of activity and time allowance
for each session, using behaviour analysis and other perceptual measures to determine the effect of each design
change. As a result we have built up considerable and
quantified design experience, giving us more precise control
over the effect of this training than we believe to be possible
with any other form of interactive skills training.

This, then, was the basic system which we had produced
and which was operational in April 1969. Our target population in BOAC was the supervisory level or its equivalent.
However, it seemed evident to us that this method would be
equally, if not more, relevant for management training. At
this juncture, Peter Honey and one of his colleagues left to
take up the opportunity to develop the system, with a
managerial level target population, in the newly formed
Management Training Unit of International Computers
Limited. Since then, there have been two separate strands
of development. In BOAC the work has continued, supported
by a research grant from the Air Transport and Travel ITB,
developing a potent and economically viable form of interactive skills training for supervisors. In ICL, systems have
been developed for changing managerial behaviour. In
both companies, an increasing concern with problems of

64 the search for
new methods in
interactive skills
training

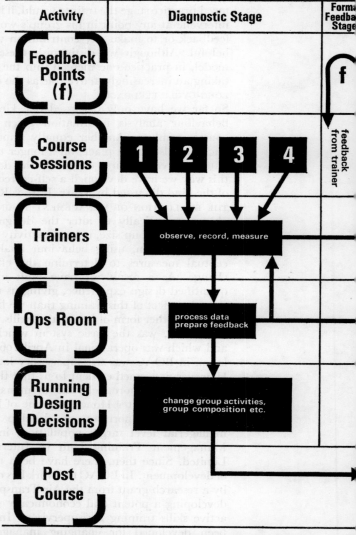

Activity	Diagnostic Stage	Formal Feedback Stage
Feedback Points (f)		**f**
Course Sessions	1 2 3 4	feedback from trainer
Trainers	observe, record, measure	
Ops Room	process data prepare feedback	
Running Design Decisions	change group activities, group composition etc.	
Post Course		

4 a model for interactive skills training

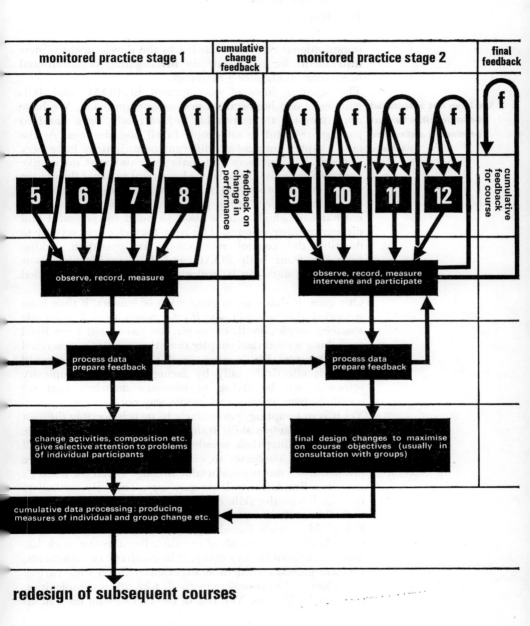

organisational relevance has led to the development of new instruments for quantitatively investigating organisational behaviour, as chapter 3 describes.

The separate lines of development in BOAC and ICL emphasise one important aspect of our approach. We have not attempted the impossible task of producing a standard package relevant to all people in all organisations. As the next chapter emphasises, different organisations have very different job interfaces and make very different interactive demands on individuals. So we have tried to avoid the golden rule fallacy by producing, not a glib answer to every trainer's interactive prayer, but a rather complex series of control mechanisms which can be used to build up powerful and diverse training systems. The next four chapters set out to describe the control mechanisms in operation, taking examples from both BOAC and ICL to illustrate how behavioural data can be collected and used in a controlled manner.

We have not attempted the impossible task of producing a standard package

Our guess is that a good proportion of readers, if they have struggled this far, will say *It's too complicated – I would like something simpler*. Well, of course, we too would have liked something a good deal simpler than the techniques described here. But real life is messy and complex and we could tackle it effectively only by facing up to its complexity squarely – not by trying to convince ourselves that we could discover an easy and simple way out.

Yet it is so tempting, particularly in such a horribly difficult area as interactive skills training, to listen to the package alchemists selling their wonderful trainer's stone which will bring golden outcomes to every organisation's interactive problems. But our uncomfortable message is that the trainer's stone is a fraud. There is no easy way. The only method to increase interactive skills effectively is through hard, complex and often tedious work.

But if this sounds forbidding, or even moralistic, there is nevertheless some crumb of comfort. Because our work has been carried out in very different in-company environments, we have gained considerable experience with a wide variety of problems. The complete method, with all its complexities, may not be for you. Yet, out of the two million data items which we have processed, and out of the numerous failures, setbacks and problems which we have faced, there may be individual aspects which are very relevant to your situation. Remember that although the various control mechanisms, as we describe them, are linked together into one complex whole, there is no logical reason why each should not be used separately. So behaviour analysis may be useful in some situations as an evaluation technique – or, as we are increasingly using it, part of a training needs analysis. Group mixing, as chapter 6 shows, can significantly improve the effectiveness of syndicate groups – and the whole thing can be worked out on the back of an envelope, without the need for an elaborate ops room. And, of course, we repeat our earlier invitation to copy and adapt, with the reminder that we have included a do-it-yourself guide to plagiarism. ✳

interface behaviour and organisational effectiveness

**NEIL RACKHAM
PETER HONEY
ROGER SUGDEN**

**The present chapter brings us one
step nearer to the actual training process
and the new methods. Interactive skills
training is concerned with the technique of
changing behaviour in the work situation.
But which behaviours need to be developed and
which behaviours are not significant in
improving company performance? Before any
training can start a decision has to be made
about which behaviours are relevant and
therefore need to be developed. This is, if you
like, the stage identified by the trainer as
ASSESSING THE TRAINING NEEDS OF THE
COMPANY.**

69 Neil Rackham
Peter Honey
Roger Sugden

What we have to get out of this part of the exercise is an agreement about which interactive behaviours we are in business to influence

'ANY TRAINING SYSTEM POWERFUL ENOUGH TO CHANGE managers' working behaviour is bound to result in greater organisational effectiveness.'

These are words which one of the authors remembers with discomfort, having asserted them a few years ago at a conference. 'Prove it!', was the laconic, and crushing, response from his audience. Neil Rackham, who now reveals himself as the guilty party, has since had ample time to reflect on his embarrassment and to wonder why he made so outrageous an assertion in the first place.

Yet this sort of assertion is alarmingly common. Attitude training, for example, usually contains a declared or implied assertion that if people's attitudes are changed, then their behaviour will change similarly – but Fishbein* and others have demonstrated that the link, if any, between attitude change and behaviour change is far too complex and ambiguous to justify such an assertion. This weakness in attitude-based training is often pointed out by people like ourselves, who are concerned with direct methods of changing behaviour. Of course, we make an equally outrageous assumption if we automatically believe that individual behaviour change has a significant correlation with organisational performance.

This is a crucial question. Unless we understand something of the relationship between behaviour and organisational effectiveness, then our attempts at behaviour change are unfocused, woolly and unlikely to tie in adequately with any defined corporate objectives. As the research literature of organisational behaviour frankly admits, the relationship between an organisation's effectiveness and the behaviour of those in it is *not completely understood*. Which, stripped of jargon dignity, means that we hardly understand it at all. If ever there was an area in need of careful research, this is it. The current upsurge of interest in Organisation Development demonstrates simultaneously the increasing importance attached to organisational behaviour, and our comparative ignorance about it when it comes to quantifiable facts.

Collecting data about how an organisation behaves is, at

* Fishbein, M and Ajzen, I. *Attitudinal variables and behaviour: three empirical studies and a theoretical re-analysis.* 1970, Washington U. Seattle, USA.

best, a difficult, expensive and time-consuming job. Even in the comparatively straightforward financial area for example, which can be measured relatively simply, it still needs a substantial organisational investment in an accountancy function to provide an accurate picture of a firm's financial behaviour. So it is hardly surprising that in the area of human behaviour, where transactions are many times more complex and irrational, we have no accurate balance sheet. Indeed, in terms of the comparative magnitude of the problem, every firm would need an impossibly large department, many times the size of its accountancy function, if it intended to analyse the behaviour of individuals and sum the effects of these behaviours into some corporate, behavioural balance sheet.

Perhaps the analogy weakens at this juncture, because behaviour is not straightforwardly additive like financial transactions or operating costs. The point is this: in order to understand completely how each individual's behaviour fits into the overall equation of organisational effectiveness, an enormous amount of investigation would be needed, well beyond the scope of any commercial or industrial company in Britain today. Evaluation of management training provides an example here. If we wish to assess, shall we say, the ultimate effects of interactive skills training on a firm, then we need to measure not only the changes in each individual's behaviour patterns before and after the training, but also the way in which these changes affect other people with whom the individual works. How do we know, without an impossibly-detailed investigation by teams of behavioural scientists, how much of the long-term change results from the training and how much from a host of other organisational factors? Just assuming that we had the resources to investigate, then our very investigation would be likely to have a significant and contaminating influence on people's behaviour. If the problem of evaluating the relatively defined organisational outcomes of specified behaviour changes is so difficult, then what chance have we of assessing the overall relationship between individual behaviour and the effectiveness of the organisation?

The enormous size and complexity of the problem certainly

explains why we understand so little about how to solve it. It also explains why so many people, both in training and in organisation development, would rather pretend that the relationship is an automatic one – that if an individual becomes more effective [in whatever terms the trainer cares to define effectiveness] then the result must be to increase the overall effectiveness of the organisation. This is a tempting fantasy, but there is general agreement among organisational specialists that reality isn't that simple. The late William Allen, for example, that brilliant organisational consultant who invented productivity bargaining with his FAWLEY BLUE BOOK, frequently pointed out the fallacies of equating individual and organisational behaviour. 'The concept of individual effectiveness,' he said, 'is totally meaningless unless seen in the context of the micro-culture in which the individual operates.'

Behavioural scientists are increasingly concerned with the effect which the climate or culture of an organisation has on those who work in it. A man may be outstandingly effective in one organisation, yet fail completely in another

Behavioural scientists are increasingly concerned with the effect which the climate or culture of an organisation has on those who work in it. A man may be outstandingly effective in one organisation, yet fail completely in another. Conversely, one organisation may bring out the best in those who work for it, and be characterised by a clarity and incisiveness at all levels, while another apparently similar organisation seems muddy and directionless, breeding disinterest and stagnation in its people. This difference in overall effectiveness is the most dramatic feature of organisational climate and the one with the most profound implications for many aspects of organisational and personnel policy.

It was once thought that the principal, if not the sole, factor in determining organisational climate was the calibre of top management

It was once thought that the principal, if not the sole, factor in determining organisational climate was the calibre of top management. An effective and capable top management was believed to ensure an effective organisation below. Recent evidence shows that the problem is more subtle and complex than this. Although a high calibre of senior management is a *necessary* condition of organisational effectiveness, it is by no means a *sufficient* condition. Even a first class top management cannot make real progress until the value system of the whole organisation is ready to accept senior management's change policies and to work with these policies rather than against them. Indeed, the greater the disparity between top management and the rest of the organisation, in terms of abilities, motivations and values, the more difficult it may be for the organisation to be effective. In a very real sense, although change in an organisation is normally initiated from the top, it will only be successful if preparation for it has gone on from below. This preparation involves bringing about systematic, and sometimes considerable, changes in the organisation's climate or, as Bill Allen put it, the micro-culture.

But how does all this tie in with a book which describes new methods for developing interactive skills? From our point of view the connection was an uncomfortable one when, having developed some interesting methods for changing individual behaviour, we realised that we had no method for determining how these behaviour changes related to the effectiveness of the organisation as a whole. So we read indigestibly-large quantities of published research and even larger quantities of rambling speculation, hoping to find helpful information which would give us some guidance. As we should have anticipated in so complex a field, what we read was confusing and contradictory. Consequently, it became very clear that if we wanted to relate our work to a wider organisational context, then we would have to develop some methods for ourselves. Needless to say, we were very discouraged at the thought. It was not the first time that we had looked round to see if we could indulge in some simple plagiarism – it hardly seemed fair that we should be out of luck yet again!

The rest of this chapter describes the way in which we explored the relationship between behaviour and organisational effectiveness. We would not pretend to have found definitive answers – indeed, one of our major findings is that such answers seem unlikely to exist. But we have developed methods of quantitatively describing organisational behaviour which we believe might be useful to other people working in training or organisation development.

The comparative importance of interactive and non-interactive behaviours in determining organisational effectiveness Because we were working with methods of changing people's interactive performance, the first question we explored was the comparative importance of interactive and non-interactive behaviours in determining organisational effectiveness. Per-

73 Neil Rackham
Peter Honey
Roger Sugden

haps a definition would be useful here. We would **define** an interactive behaviour as one which involves two or more people in such a way that the behaviour of one person may influence the behaviour of others. So discussion, in its many forms, is clearly an important class of interactive behaviour. Similarly, certain less direct forms of interaction, such as telephone conversations, would constitute interactive behaviour. Memos, letters, plans and the like are a grey area. Their preparation, if it does not involve any other person, is non-interactive – although they may have important interactive consequences. For example, we have recorded a case in the engineering industry where a production manager wrote the following memo to his senior foreman

I have agreed that we shall treat type C gears as having maximum priority in No 3 Machine Bay until outstanding orders for July are cleared. Please make sure that this is done.

The production of this memo, by our definition, was non-interactive in that the manager wrote it alone. But within two hours of sending it, we recorded a total of 34 sets of interactions between people as priorities in the machine shop were reset and the work loading was altered to cope with the manager's instructions. Management is a particularly interactive occupation and it is therefore not surprising that even the non-interactive behaviours may have interactive consequences.

Another way to look at interactive behaviour is to consider it as behaviour which takes place at the interface between jobs Another way to look at interactive behaviour is to consider it as behaviour which takes place at the interface between jobs, rather than within individual job boundaries. We have increasingly come to use the term INTERFACE BEHAVIOUR when describing the interactions between people on the job: How important are these interactions, or interfaces? Our little machine shop example certainly indicates that interface behaviours are frequent, but how do they relate to individual and organisational effectiveness?

On the individual level, the evidence is convincing. We asked a sample of over 100 middle and junior managers, *How much of your job effectiveness is determined exclusively by your own actions and how much is determined by your interactions with other people?* Their consensus was that between 85 and 90 per cent of their effectiveness depended on their interaction with others.

A more objective piece of evidence was quoted in the previous chapter. Using a Critical Incident technique with supervisors from the chemical industry, it was discovered that the majority of problems faced by each supervisor, in terms of both frequency and severity, were interactive. This sort of evidence, which shows that individual effectiveness is largely dependent on interface behaviour, is plentiful. There will be very few individuals reading this chapter whose effectiveness is not primarily dependent on their interfaces with other people.

However, when it comes to the relationship between interface behaviour and overall organisational effectiveness, the evidence is more difficult to obtain and more ambiguous in its interpretation. We were able to get part way there in a study of work groups. We found that when we examined six work groups whose performance was rated by management as below average, there was a significantly greater number of interface problems in each group than in similar groups which management had rated as either average or above average. However, in only two of the six groups was there significant evidence that individuals were below average in their non-interactive performance. So, in terms of small groups of individuals, the importance of interface behaviour in determining group effectiveness is not too difficult to establish.

In overall organisational terms, the interface characteristics are more complex. And it is not just a question of scale. **Within an organisation, many interfaces have key organisational, as well as behavioural, characteristics**. So an identical behaviour can have very different consequences in different organisational settings. The managing director who tells a junior clerk to get out of his sight is generally indulging in a less risky interface behaviour than the junior clerk who addresses his managing director in similar terms. And organisational difficulties can exaggerate the behaviour problems at any interface. So, for example, it is common for maintenance and production functions, because of the way they may relate organisationally, to be at each other's throats behaviourally.

In short, the effectiveness of any interface behaviour in an organisation is clearly dependent on many more factors than the simple behaviour itself. However, within each organisation, there is likely to be a number of identifiable behaviours which are seen by members of that organisation as acceptable, appropriate and generally associated with effectiveness. These patterns of acceptable behaviour constitute the micro-culture, or organisational climate. Because it is the organisational climate of a firm which distinguishes it behaviourally from other organisations, a technique for analysing organisational climate is important in any attempt to bring about purposive organisational change.

Many people have ignored organisational climate and they have usually suffered for doing so. The history of organisational disasters is rich in examples. A common, and dangerous, form of disregard is the package approach, where a change policy is mechanistically applied irrespective of organisational circumstances. As the previous chapter discussed, interactive skills training packages are notorious in this respect.

We don't suggest that organisational climate is ignored by choice. On the contrary, most of those people who work in organisational change situations are full of good intentions in this respect. Their difficulty is that they cannot take organisational climate into account because they have no way of assessing it. Some people are said to have a **feel** for these differences in organisational culture. To quote Bill Allen again

> *The best management consultants, and there can only be a handful of such people in this country, are distinguished by their immediate sensitivity to the different micro-cultures in which they operate: and they use these cultural differences to great advantage.*

However, there are obvious snags in relying on this intuitive approach. For one thing, lots of people **think** that they understand organisational climate – and that may be dangerous because, as Bill Allen pointed out, only a handful of people actually possess this capacity. And if a top-level consultant is needed to look at the organisational culture

They cannot take organisational climate into account because they have no way of assessing it

and its constituent interface behaviours, then it may be a prohibitively expensive business.

We were convinced that the answer to the problem lay in measurement. If we could develop an economical, quantifiable and statistically sound method for measuring organisational climate, then we would be able to identify some of the key behaviours which were associated with organisational effectiveness. We would then be in a position to judge the behaviour changes resulting from our training methods in terms of the key organisational behaviours revealed by our analysis.

The general method which was adopted in both BOAC and ICL, was to compare the behaviour of individuals who were considered by management to be very effective, with the behaviour of individuals who were considered as very ineffective. In this way we were able to isolate those behaviours which management associated with effectiveness. To take a very simple example, suppose we discovered that all those individuals judged by their managers as effective spoke loudly and that all those judged as ineffective spoke softly, then we would conclude that having a loud voice was associated with effectiveness in that particular organisational culture.

Our basic method was a simple one. If we found that a behaviour was common in one of the effectiveness groups but not in the other, then we inferred that this behaviour was, in some way, related to perceived organisational effectiveness. Notice how the word **perceived** has cropped up in the previous sentence. In this context we were much more interested in behaviour perceived as effective than we were in behaviour which could be objectively related to effectiveness. Organisational climate is, after all, the firm's value system – and values are to do with beliefs and perceptions, not with objective facts. However, we shall return to the relationship between fact and belief later in the chapter. This basic method was applied in very different ways within BOAC and ICL, so here the story diverges.

In BOAC our specific concern was the way in which supervisors' interface behaviour was affected by the organisational climate in which they worked. We constructed an 86-item

Organisational climate is, after all, the firm's value system – and values are to do with beliefs and perceptions, not with objective facts

77 Neil Rackham
Peter Honey
Roger Sugden

questionnaire, which consisted of items taken from our own
organisational experience elsewhere, from behavioural
science sources [readers who know the Ohio leadership
research studies, for example, would detect half a dozen
items in common] and from the experience of Mike Colbert
and his team in BOAC General Training Department. Some
randomly chosen examples from the final questionnaire are

Q5   Is his technical knowledge

- [ ] very good
- [ ] good
- [ ] moderate
- [ ] poor
- [ ] very poor

Q40   Does he accept responsibility
for his people's mistakes?

- [ ] always
- [ ] often
- [ ] occasionally
- [ ] seldom
- [ ] never

Q77   Does he tend to work in
isolation?

- [ ] always
- [ ] often
- [ ] occasionally
- [ ] seldom
- [ ] never

A representative sample of 95 BOAC managers was asked,
without naming any individual, to rate their most effective
subordinate in terms of the 86 behaviour characteristics of
the questionnaire. They were then asked to rate their least
effective subordinate similarly. So, from each manager, we
obtained two completed questionnaires, one rating the most
effective and the other rating the least effective of those
working for him. By comparing the average ratings of the
most effective and least effective groups, those characteristics
which BOAC managers associated with effective performance
were isolated. Differences between various areas of BOAC
were also analysed. A similar survey was carried out with a
sample of 65 managers from BOAC Canada and USA.

Before discussing the results we should make one point clear. Our purpose in this chapter is to describe a method, rather than to discuss the organisational climate of BOAC. We shall therefore select our results to illuminate the method rather than the organisation.

The first analysis of the data was simple: we looked at each item to see whether the group who were rated as effective showed more, or less, of that particular behaviour than the group rated as ineffective. [For the technically minded, because a large number of items were showing significant differences between groups, we used a rather strict series of statistical tests before declaring an item as significant. Stuart Smith, of Sheffield Polytechnic, devised a programme which gave us t tests, Wilcoxon test, sign test and a special polarity-based test which he produced for us. We did not declare any item as significant unless it passed at least two out of the four tests.]

The way in which this item-by-item analysis gave us information can be seen by looking at the questionnaire examples which we have already taken.

Q5 Technical knowledge showed that in the more technical areas of BOAC, such as the engineering function, both the most effective and the least effective supervisors had a very high level of technical knowledge – so it seemed that technical knowledge did not, in itself differentiate the effective supervisor. However, in the less technical areas, such as the commercial function, the level of technical knowledge of the most effective supervisors was significantly greater than for the least effective group.

Q40 Accepting responsibility for his people's mistakes this behaviour was very significantly associated with effectiveness in all areas of BOAC. However, in the USA it was slightly less associated than in other areas.

Q77 Works in isolation the least effective supervisors worked in isolation significantly more than did supervisors from the most effective group. However, there were very considerable individual differences for this question, with the effective supervisors from particular areas sometimes working in isolation more than their ineffective colleagues.

Analysing each question in this way gave us some insights into the individual behaviours associated with supervisory effectiveness. As a result we could tell a certain amount about the overall organisational climate and differences between certain geographical or functional areas. For example, we found that in the USA, the effective supervisor was significantly less likely to trust his people to do a good job, or to complain of having too much to do, or to give his people the opportunity to rectify their mistakes, than effective supervisors in Canada or the UK.

Data from individual questions also gave us an indication of the relevance of the behaviour changes which were resulting from our new training methods. For example, one of the behaviour categories which showed a consistent and significant increase in frequency during our training was BUILDING, which we defined as a behaviour which developed somebody else's ideas further. One of our questions in the original behaviour survey was, *Does he develop other people's ideas?* We found that the effective supervisors developed the ideas of others significantly more than did the less effective group. So it would be fair to conclude that the increase in BUILDING behaviour resulting from our training would be generally seen by the 160 managers in our study as organisationally appropriate.

Not all of the changes which occurred during training were in line with the results from the Organisation Behaviour Survey. For example, CRITICISING was a behaviour category which, we felt, was likely to be correlated with poor interface behaviour. Our guess was that supervisors who indulged in the most criticism of other people were likely to create friction which would reduce their interface effectiveness. We were therefore most satisfied to find that during training the overall number of CRITICISING contributions dropped very significantly as the course progressed. However, we **There were** included a number of questions about criticising behaviour **circumstances where a** in the survey and none of them showed the overall relation- **very high level of** ship with ineffectiveness which we would have predicted. **criticising behaviour** In fact, in our USA group, there were circumstances where **was associated with** a very high level of criticising behaviour was associated with **effectiveness** effectiveness.

This, of course, confirms Bill Allen's view that an individual's effectiveness can be judged only in the context of his environment or micro-culture. Our analysis of each question showed us that the value system of the training, which encouraged open, frank and constructive interactions between people, was more clearly associated with effectiveness in some areas of BOAC than in others. In fact, it was possible to construct a sort of league table comparing each area of BOAC in terms of similarity between the values of the training and the values of the organisational climate.

But this may sound very abstract and theoretical. What implications does it have for training? If our arguments have been sound, then we would expect that the training would be seen as most effective in those areas where there was a high compatibility between the values of the training and the values of that part of the BOAC micro-culture. In areas where the changes resulting from the training were not seen as associated with effectiveness then, irrespective of how useful we trainers believed these changes to be, we would predict that the training would be perceived as ineffective. This prediction, fortunately, could easily be tested. During the training, after each of the 30 or so sessions, course members were asked to rate the session in terms of a number of criteria, including relevance to their jobs, using a seven-point scale. We would predict that those course members coming from an organisational climate whose values were in line with those of the training would perceive the training as more relevant to their jobs than would course members coming from an area where there was little compatibility between the organisational climate and the training values. FIGURE 5 shows how our predictions were confirmed.

So one clear use of the organisation behaviour survey is to give us a much-needed measure for checking whether a particular form of training is compatible with the values of the organisation. With this information we can decide how to spend our training resources more effectively, knowing which parts of the organisation will respond best

81 Neil Rackham
Peter Honey
Roger Sugden

5 applicability of training to different parts of the organisation

behaviour survey area	average applicability rating by 20 participants from area (maximum 7)
area with the highest compatibility between survey values and training values	5·1
area with the least compatibility between survey values and training values	2·7
average of all other areas	4·2

We can design new forms of training specifically adapted to overall company need

to particular forms of interactive skills training. And, more important, knowing the significant differences in behaviours seen as effective in different companies – or, as in the case of a large corporation such as BOAC, between various parts of a company – we can design new forms of training specifically adapted either to overall company need or to the individual needs of particular areas within large organisations. In one sense, our information may be misleading. For instance, take the questionnaire item we have already discussed, which asked about technical knowledge. This showed us that effective supervisors in all parts of BOAC were perceived as having a very high level of technical knowledge. In this respect, effective supervisors in North America were very similar in level to effective supervisors in Britain, so this question told us nothing about any differences between these two areas of the organisation. However, using a rather more sophisticated statistical technique called cluster analysis, we were able to get extra, and revealing information out of results like this. Cluster analysis is, in simple terms, a way of finding which items go together. So, in our technical knowledge example, cluster analysis showed that in the UK, the cluster of behaviours concerned with job knowledge was as follows

In the training world we know, often to our cost, that training programmes which are highly successful in one environment may prove to be the most embarrassing flops when applied to apparently similar situations elsewhere

good technical knowledge

good overall knowledge of job

displays technical competence in job

good technical knowledge

6 job knowledge cluster UK

The deeper you wish to probe the harder it becomes to explain your procedures and findings to line managers

good overall knowledge of job

not over-concerned with unnecessary detail

While in North America we found

7 job knowledge cluster USA and Canada

83 Neil Rackham
Peter Honey
Roger Sugden

So it seems that there is a difference after all. In the UK, a high level of general and technical job knowledge is, in itself, perceived to be associated with effectiveness. In North America, however, job knowledge is associated with overall effectiveness only when it is actually displayed or put into practice, and when it does not lead to over-concern with unnecessary detail. In the UK therefore, because knowledge is seen as a good thing in itself, the knowledgeable supervisor will, other things being equal, be perceived as more effective than his less knowledgeable colleagues, irrespective of whether he is seen to put his knowledge into practice. But

The North American manager has much less respect for pure knowledge

the North American manager has much less respect for pure knowledge. He associates knowledge with effectiveness only when there is evidence that this knowledge is being applied successfully to the supervisors' jobs. This is, of course, one of the differences which is popularly supposed to exist between the industrial cultures of Britain and North America.

Our survey produced further differences between the British and North American areas which might reflect deeper national values. In the USA, for example, the following cluster is associated with supervisory effectiveness.

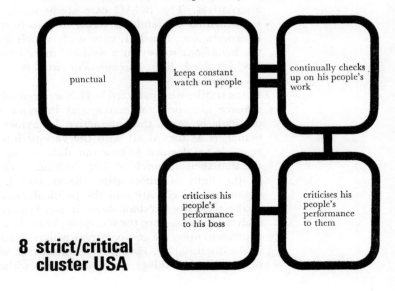

8 strict/critical cluster USA

Sociologists have often commented on the strong influence in the United States of the Protestant Ethic, which embodies the values expressed in this cluster. Nothing of the sort emerged in either the UK or the Canadian study and none of the individual behaviours in this cluster was significantly associated with effectiveness except in the United States.

By using cluster analysis techniques it is possible to get beyond individual behaviours into the more complex, more exciting, areas of managerial and organisational style. Unfortunately, the deeper you wish to probe, the more necessary it becomes to possess special skills in statistics, questionnaire design and so forth. And the harder it becomes to explain your procedures and findings to line managers. Even Organisation Development specialists are rarely qualified to carry out this kind of work. So we have been faced with an awkward problem. Should we push ahead with very sophisticated methods of investigation which could be carried out only by behavioural scientists, or should we keep to rather more direct methods which could involve line management at every stage of the planning, data collecting and interpreting process? We have explored both alternatives. The BOAC case study made comparatively sophisticated demands in terms of statistical methods and interpretation. The ICL case study which follows has used the behaviour survey in a simpler, more direct, way which has involved line management at every stage of the investigation.

In the studies we conducted in ICL we decided to concentrate massive attention on managerial interface situations and particularly upon the interactive behaviour displayed by managers as they dealt with the various interfaces. In this example we decided to base our data on the perceptions of the managers themselves. The decision to do so was made in the light of information about the openness of the organisational climate and the political anxieties prevalent at the time. As we shall show, it was important to bow to such constraints, since the success of the study was particularly dependent upon the co-operative involvement of the managers in the organisation. However, it meant that we were unable to do a lot of things we would have wished to do. For example the information we assembled about managerial behaviour was anonymous. This meant that we automatically denied ourselves access to indices of effectiveness, which we could correlate with the interface behaviours we uncovered. Also, the information was one-way, in the sense that the study involved managers giving data about their immediate subordinate level of management but not vice versa. And, finally, the climate at that time meant that we could not do much direct interface observing ourselves.

Given, then, that we were so dependent on the behaviours which were **perceived** as being closely associated with effectiveness, what could usefully be done? Throughout the description which follows it is vital to remain clear about what we were trying to achieve. Our purposes were threefold:

● To discover which interactive behaviours, if any, were perceived as being closely associated with managerial effectiveness and to distinguish them from behaviours associated with ineffectiveness – we found it less emotive to talk about less effective rather than ineffective during the initial stages of our work.

● In the light of the significant distinguishing behaviours, to identify which behaviours were appropriate and which inappropriate in the context of the organisational culture or climate. This meant that we were able to select the interactive behaviours which were to determine the ingredients of the subsequent training programme in full knowledge, and relative certainty, that they would be reinforced by the organisational climate, rather than obliterated by it.

● Whilst achieving these two purposes, to achieve a third of a rather different nature. Namely, to involve all the managers in the organisation in a real rather than apparent way, in order that their participation in these investigatory phases might lead to willing and purposeful attendance on the eventual training programmes.

So far we have been using the term *the organisation* quite glibly, as though all 35 000 members of ICL were embraced by our study. In fact, the studies undertaken within ICL have all coped with one sub-part of the total organisation at a time. So, for example, the first study was carried out in the UK sales organisation which is about two thousand people strong, and a later study took place in the servicing organisation which has a total staff of about five thousand. Tackling the organisation in this way, bit by bit, has helped us to become more thorough in understanding the various sub-cultures operating in the total organisational system and has highlighted important sub-cultural differences.

The first step in the studies was designed to combine purposes one and three. It seemed to us that if we were on a quest to discover interactive behaviours which were perceived as being associated with effectiveness, and that if we wanted to involve managers to the hilt in our various activities, then the sensible thing to do was to get the managers themselves to come up with the bulk of the questionnaire material. Accordingly, we gathered them together in a series of small groups and posed the question, *How do effective managers in this part of the organisation behave?* They were asked to fix their thoughts on a manager they judged effective and to start describing his behaviour in interactive and interface situations. They were not required to identify people, nor were they asked to justify anything they came up with. Pressure was applied only when they came up with global descriptive statements at the level of managerial qualities or attributes. When, for example, they came up with things like *He is decisive, a good leader, has confidence,* they would be halted and each item would be probed in order to analyse it into a series of specific behaviours. Questions like, *What is it about his overt behaviour which leads you to conclude that he is a good leader?* and *What does he actually do which earns him that description?* were very useful in breaking down descriptive statements into more precise behavioural elements.

These sessions would last for an hour or so. Sometimes we tape-recorded the conversations, sometimes a girl took down the main points verbatim in shorthand. We were careful to include virtually all the managers in this step and found that they enjoyed the experience. Most managers would go out of their way to remark about the excitement and

Tackling the organisation in this way, bit by bit, has helped us to become more thorough in understanding the various sub-cultures

rigour of thinking through to specific situational behaviours. We then assembled the material thus collected into an unvalidated questionnaire. The amount of editorial work was kept to a sensible minimum. We would put the items into a respectable questionnaire format, but with as little tampering with the wording of each item as possible. The actual format of questionnaire construction has varied, though we have tended to prefer semantic differential scales, with items poled between a five or seven-point scale. A typical questionnaire produced in this way has upwards of one hundred poled behavioural items.

With the questionnaire in existence, the next step was to conduct the survey itself. We topped and tailed our way through the organisation by getting each manager to complete two questionnaires; one with the behaviour of his most effective subordinate manager in mind and, on a separate occasion, a second questionnaire, consisting of the same items, with the behaviour of his least effective subordinate manager in mind. This meant that, as in the BOAC studies, we were able to compare the average ratings of the most effective and least effective groups and to determine which items were truly significant in distinguishing between the two groups.

One point perhaps worth making in passing is that we resisted the temptation to conduct this survey through the internal mailing system. Bearing in mind our purposes to do with people feeling involved and interested, we went to the trouble [fairly considerable too, since the managers were geographically spread throughout the UK] of taking the questionnaire to them in person. This had the advantage of standardising the conditions under which each questionnaire blank was completed, besides being on the spot to cope with queries and to amplify the design and purpose of the exercise as appropriate. It is also a great way to guarantee a 100 per cent response!

The items which survived the statistical analysis were the significant distinguishing interactive behaviours which we needed to isolate in order to agree what behaviour changes were appropriate.

Examples of some of our findings in one part of ICL are
● Effective managers check that people have understood
them whereas less effective managers assume that they
have been understood.
● Effective managers tend to go to their bosses with
proposals and plans of action, whereas less effective
managers come up with problems and difficulties.
● Effective managers set specific, explicit objectives and
standards for their people, where the less effective
managers set less explicit and more general objectives,
and no standards.
● Effective managers admit it when things are not going
so well, whereas the less effective manager tends to make
defensive explanations and to whitewash reality.
Findings like these gave us the sort of insight into the
organisational climate that we had to have if we were to
embark upon a behaviour change programme which was
consonant with the value system. Furthermore, and perhaps
this is a much more important point, the results were vitally
useful in giving the managers in the organisations a clear
mirror image of their interactive culture. We fed back the
behaviours which were significant distinguishers in a series
of meetings where the implications, particularly in terms of
the achievement of the organisation's commercial objectives,
were explored. In our experience, managers find it an unusual, yet worthwhile, experience to examine the relationships between behavioural means and commercial ends.
The object of such deliberations goes beyond sheer fascina-
tion with the data, however. What we have to get out of it
is agreement about which interactive behaviours we are in
business to influence. In our ICL work we have been keen
to help the managers themselves to sort out what they want
to get out of the training programme. Once we have been
furnished with objectives and standards, we can then turn
our professional attention to the design of the change
programme itself. And we can do this secure in the knowledge
that its objectives are appropriate to the organisational
climate and that the managers within it have already made
considerable investments in the success of the training.
The usefulness of the organisation behaviour survey extends

**Managers find it
an unusual,
yet worthwhile,
experience to examine
the relationships
between behavioural
means and commercial
ends**

89 Neil Rackham
Peter Honey
Roger Sugden

beyond training and much of this usefulness derives, para-doxically enough, from the behaviour survey's capacity to measure beliefs and not facts. Let us take an example. Management succession, or the promotion system, is being studied increasingly carefully and objectively by most large companies. Promising junior people are discovered by scientific selection methods, given carefully-controlled managerial experience and then placed to fill a selected management vacancy. With all this care and objectivity, it would seem very unlikely that planned succession could result in serious mistakes. Unfortunately, such mistakes are relatively frequent. And the main cause, in our experience, is that the whole succession programme is based on a system which, in its desire to be objective, has excluded all consideration of organisational climate.

Organisation behaviour surveys gain a great deal of information about the promotion channel Organisation behaviour surveys, in asking for managers' perceptions of their most effective subordinates, are also gaining a great deal of information concerning managers' views about the promotion channel. It is, after all, the subordinate you feel to be most effective that you normally recommend for promotion. So the key behaviours emerging from the survey give a clear idea of management's concept of promotability. We know from the survey work described in this article, that the sort of person considered highly promotable in ICL is very different in his behaviour from his highly-promotable counterpart in BOAC. Differences of this sort may explain why carefully-designed succession systems work less effectively when applied to organisations other than the ones for which they were originally developed. One of the authors investigated 20 cases where people who had been placed in a job as a result of a management succession programme had performed so badly that they either had been removed or their position was under review. In 14 of these cases, the most important reason for the individual's poor performance was not lack of ability or training but, as one line manager put it 'a failure to fit into the niche that people had carved out for him'. Our way of expressing this would be to say that in 14 out of 20 cases promotion took insufficient account of the organisational climate.

But, and this is a vital question, how much account of organisational climate **should** we take? The answer is a question of balance. It would be stupid to base decisions solely on the values of the existing organisational climate – there would be no quicker way to ensure stagnation and bankruptcy. If the belief system of the organisation is against change, for example, and sees all change-oriented behaviour as ineffective, then to accept this and design training and selection systems to minimise change would be a dangerous aquiescence to an unhealthy organisational climate. However, to ignore the organisation's value system in similar circumstances would be equally foolhardy. Introducing change agents to a system deeply opposed to change requires a very different strategy from introducing them in an organisational climate where change is readily accepted. Lack of knowledge about organisational climate puts a severe constraint on most organisation development activities. How can we select effectively without any idea of the organisational acceptability of our selection? And how safe is it to assume that the criteria for promotion in one organisation will be applicable to other companies, or to other areas within large corporations? In the training world we know, often to our cost, that training programmes which are highly successful in one environment may prove to be the most embarrassing flops when applied to apparently similar situations elsewhere. When we turn to the more complex field of organisation development, how can we operate any system effectively unless we have some measure of the overall organisational climate which we hope to develop? It is of very little use producing powerful forms of training to change individual behaviour unless we can relate that change to some overall organisational policy. As behaviour change training becomes more powerful, so this becomes an increasingly pressing problem.

And that brings us back to our initial question about the relationship between individual behaviour and the effectiveness of the organisation. Our argument has been that each individual's behaviour can be judged only in a context. And we call that context ORGANISATIONAL CLIMATE. Unless we can relate our activities in selection, promotion and

91 Neil Rackham
Peter Honey
Roger Sugden

training to the overall organisational climate, then we are working in a vacuum. And a vacuum is a dangerously empty place in which to work. ✳

chapter 4

INTERACTIVE SKILLS

collecting
behavioural
data

MICHAEL J COLBERT BOAC
MICHAEL MORRIS ICL
STEPHEN TRIBE BOAC

I suppose most of us in the training world would subscribe to the principle that WHAT YOU CANNOT MEASURE YOU CANNOT CONTROL

93 Michael J Colbert
Michael Morris
Stephen Tribe

AS TRAINING IS NOTHING LESS THAN A BID TO CONTROL learning, the implication for trainers is inescapable: if we want to establish control over the learning process, then we need, as a basic requirement, to measure what is being learned in any training situation we care to design – we need to measure as best we can the behaviour changes brought about by the training. Only when we have collected such behavioural data are we in any sort of position to start focusing the training towards meeting defined individual and organisational needs.

Every evaluative effort made to improve the effectiveness of training needs to involve the collection of behavioural data

Thus every evaluative effort made to improve the effectiveness of training – such as the one described in these chapters – needs to involve the collection of behavioural data – it's our raw material! The value of such raw material as a source of feedback to both trainee and trainer will of course depend upon how well we measure: the more sensitive and reliable the measures the greater the degree of control achievable.

Raw material or not, it's hard to come by in the sort of training we're talking about. It is this lack of data on the behavioural changes brought about by the training that, more than any other single factor, makes existing methods employed in interactive skills training so unconvincing.

Why this lack of behavioural data – this raw material of ours? The fact that such an unsatisfactory situation persists is worth exploring: if only to provide some insight into the sort of problems faced by anyone who attempts to collect such data!

To begin with, in probably no other area of training is data collection – the prerequisite of control – more obviously difficult than in the various forms of interactive skills training where group interaction is used as a vehicle for learning. The enormous variety, speed, subtlety and complexity of interactions within a training group – or any group for that matter – is such that even an experienced observer has difficulty in remembering more than a small proportion of them. Even then, the little an observer remembers is unlikely to be wholly representative of the welter of interactions that occurred within the group because of the influence of perceptual filters. The problem is compounded, and these difficulties pale into insignificance, when the observer then attempts to place values upon the behaviours that go to make up any interaction.

Not surprisingly – as one subsumes the other – all this is just as difficult as attempting to apply sensitive and reliable measures to managerial performance and behaviour. So difficult, in fact, that in a sense it may seem to be a case of trying to quantify the unquantifiable!

As though this wasn't enough, progress in overcoming the inherent difficulty of collecting behavioural data tends to be inhibited by the reluctance of some trainers to try. Justification for such inactivity is sometimes made on the grounds that any attempt would in all probability fall short of perfection. It most certainly would but how else will progress be made?

More generally of course such inertia, tinged as it is with a touch of fatalism, sometimes results in developments in training being judged against criteria seldom, if ever, applied to existing, accepted forms of training.

Apart from the inherent difficulty of collecting behavioural data and the inertia factor, the lack of such data may stem in part from some misconceptions about evaluation. From what has already been said, it can be deduced that for us evaluation is the systematic collection and utilisation of data in order to improve training. The feedback function implicit in this approach has been shown to have value in helping the trainee to improve his performance and the trainer to improve the design of the training. It follows that such an approach to evaluation places a premium upon the monitoring of trainee performance – the collection of behavioural data. **This is treating evaluation as an integral part of the training process.**

Unless approached in this way, evaluation tends to become detached from the training process – in the shape of evaluation studies, ad hoc pieces of research or simple measures of effectiveness. Suffice it to say that such activities tend to generate little in the way of behavioural data.

Last but not least, data collection is hard work – and not all that exciting!

Notwithstanding these various difficulties and factors – and there are others – much that passes as management

The feedback function implicit in this approach has been shown to have value in helping the trainee to improve his performance

95 Michael J Colbert
Michael Morris
Stephen Tribe

training will remain unsatisfactory and unconvincing unless interactive skills training can be given a useful data base.

Turning from the general to the particular, it is significant that the development of the training described in this book effectively dates from the time – in 1968 – when we began to measure what was happening within training groups on the early BOAC courses.

A number of systems designed to record, categorise and measure interactions between members of a group were available and of these we employed the Bales Interaction Analysis and the Haynes Task-Centred Analysis – supported by video tape recordings. The results of this early effort in measuring are given by Neil Rackham in an earlier chapter and only one of the findings need concern us here. It was the realisation that the measuring instruments – particularly the Bales Analysis – were inadequate in that they were failing to detect what appeared to be important behaviour changes.

Although fundamentally important contributions to the study of group behaviour, it was apparent that, being general instruments, they were not particularly suited to interactive skills training. After digesting the disturbing implications of this and other findings to do with the training we realised – albeit hesitantly – that if we were to get anywhere we had little option but to develop a new system of categorising behaviour. In developing a new BEHAVIOUR ANALYSIS system the following criteria of usefulness were identified and employed

● a chosen category must describe a behaviour which can change during the course of training
● it must differentiate between categories
● categories must be meaningful both to group members and to trainers
● it must permit a high inter-rater reliability when used by members of the training staff

The third criterion derived from the need to be able to produce behaviour measures which would – without too much difficulty – provide the basis for meaningful feedback to those observed. Bales method, in particular, suffers from the lack of comprehension which training groups have about

the operational definition of categories such as *negative
socio-emotional behaviour*. This is exemplified by the time
needed by observers of training groups to achieve satisfactory
performance in carrying out behaviour analyses. For the
Bales scheme as long as three months has been quoted as an
apprentice period before observers, usually with a behavioural
science background, become sufficiently reliable to be usable
in the training situation.

This leads us on to the fourth criterion and some of its
implications. Our intention has always been to develop a
system of interactive skills training, and specifically a
behaviour analysis framework, which could be used, under
supervision, by the training or personnel manpower of the
average sophisticated company – with minimal training.
T-Groups and the like, whatever their relevancy for business
organisations, have been hindered in their growth by the
shortage of very qualified, skilled and expensive personnel
needed to control them.

So, armed with video tapes of groups at various stages of
the task-centred interactive skills training courses being run
in BOAC, the work of developing a new system of behaviour
analysis began. Thorough analysis of the tapes identified
27 behaviour categories which seemed promising. With the
help of trials and the development of the criteria of usefulness,
mentioned earlier on, these were whittled down to a
manageable eleven

● **helpful proposing**
● **unhelpful proposing**
● **supporting**
● **disagreeing**
● **building**
● **criticising**
● **clarifying**
● **confusing**
● **systematic**
● **other behaviour judged appropriate**
● **other behaviour judged inappropriate**

Thus by early 1969 these categories, each with an agreed
operational definition, formed the basis of our new behaviour
analysis (BA). Although the subsequent experience and

97 Michael J Colbert
Michael Morris
Stephen Tribe

systematic development in both BOAC and ICL revealed its limitations, this first BA gave us the chance to collect the sort of behavioural data we needed. At last we had some chance of bringing the training under control.

For those unfamiliar with measuring instruments such as the BA, a brief word about the mechanics of recording the data. Using the categories that figured in the original BA, a simple piece of conversation, and a basic method of categorisation, each person's contributions could be categorised

Mary 'I think we should let them know.' *Helpful proposal*
Joe 'That's a good idea. Let's do that.' *Supporting*
Mary 'Fine. I'll ring them now.' *Building*
Bill 'Not likely!' *Disagreeing*

Given the two constraints – that of recording a behaviour against a person – there is little room for variation in the design of a BA form. Typically, an observer would record this snatch of conversation on a form like this

9

Categories	Names		
	Mary	Bill	Joe
Helpful Proposals	I		
Supporting			I
Disagreeing		I	
Building	I		

For the purposes of this example other categories and group members have not been listed.

Given that this was the starting point, let us now look at the way in which the system of behaviour analysis has subsequently developed in ICL and BOAC.

BEHAVIOUR ANALYSIS DEVELOPMENT IN ICL

The behaviour analysis sheet shown in FIGURE 10 is an example of one format currently and often used in ICL. Before looking at current practice, a short review of the evolution of the process may set the scene usefully without dwelling too long in the past.

The introductory part of this chapter has shown the advantages, from several points of view, of the behaviour analysis approach to data collection. Having once lighted upon the methodology, we began on an experimental trail toward making our data collection tool useful. In this context useful means quite a few things. Here are some of the main requirements of successful behaviour analysis

● it must be a distinguisher of behaviours that actually matter to the group situation

● it must be seen by delegates as comprehensible, reliable and relevant

● it must pick up behaviours that are susceptible to development and change

Since we began, there have been several inputs to the design and refinement of behaviour analysis and its categories. In the earliest period after launching behaviour analysis our prime source of information was our own imagination or, to be fairer to ourselves, our own experience of the behaviours significant to the interpersonal behaviour of managers. Field investigation into the behaviours associated with managerial effectiveness, and its opposite, enabled us to confirm some of our thinking, but with a basis of much more objective information to refine and change categories. The subject of surveying is covered in another chapter, so suffice it to say here that not the least benefit gained has been in enhancing the credibility of the whole process to managers in training.

The third major input to the development of behaviour analysis has been our own experience of its use and practicability. Like BOAC, we once tried a category called *systematic behaviour*. The snag that appeared in practice was that no one seemed in the event to be able to say with any precision what was systematic and what was not. We have tried distinguishing helpful and unhelpful behaviours. Once we

99 Michael J Colbert
Michael Morris
Stephen Tribe

10 behaviour analysis ICL

Task No: 26   Description: Undertake an activity that the group agrees will serve a useful purpose

Start time: 14.50   Finish time: 15.35   Any time absent: None

	DON	PETER	JOHN	DAVID	JIM	BILL	MIKE
SEEKING SUGGESTIONS (ideas and proposals)	卌 卌 II	I	II	(III	II		I
CAUGHT PROPOSALS	III	卌 II	卌 卌	(II	IIII	卌 卌 卌 II	卌 卌 卌 III
ESCAPED PROPOSALS	I	I	I	IIII	卌 III	II	I
BUILDING	I	I			III		
DISAGREEING and CRITICISING	III	卌 III	卌 卌 II	(III	II	卌 I	III
SEEKING CONFIRMATION (agreement and support)	卌 卌 卌 I	III	卌 卌 I	III	II	III	卌 卌 II
SUPPORTING	II	II		卌 卌 I	卌 IIII	III	卌 卌
SEEKING CLARIFICATION EXPLANATION AND INFORMATION	卌 卌 卌 II	卌 卌 卌	卌 卌 I	卌 II	卌 卌	III	II I
OTHER BEHAVIOUR (including providing info. and explanations in response to requests)	卌 IIII	卌 卌 II	卌 卌 II	卌 卌 卌	卌 卌 II	卌 I	卌 卌 卌 卌
OFFERING (uninvited) EXPLANATIONS, REASONS and DIFFICULTIES	II	卌 卌 I	卌 卌 卌 卌	卌	III	III	卌 II
UNSTRUCTURED CONTRIBUTIONS (thinking aloud, rambling on and contradicting oneself, etc.)	II	卌	I	I	卌	III	IIII
MULTI-SPEAK (Talking over and interrupting)	卌 卌 I	卌 II	卌 卌 卌	卌 III	II	I	卌 卌 卌 卌 II

split all the categories into these two subsets to show, for example, whether a proposal was one or the other. The snags showed up quickly in practice: is a suggestion helpful because it is in some way inherently good, or because it works or because it gets listened to? Objectivity slips away quickly when the responsibility for making qualitative judgments of that kind is loaded on to the trainer. Similarly, we found that regarding one group of behaviours as helpful and another as unhelpful did not work. Proposing may look, on the face of it, like a good thing. But is it, when a radical proposal is launched into group work so late in the day that it cannot possibly be actioned and serves only to depress with the thought of opportunity lost?

Our current practice is a distillation of a lot of practical experience. Let's leave the past and have a look at some of our current work.

The behaviour categories shown in the example are in some cases virtually self-explanatory. Others probably require some commentary, and perhaps notes on a few will help illustrate the degree of specificity they achieve

Caught/escaped proposals Proposals are usually fairly easy to recognise and are often signalled in advance by 'I propose/suggest that . . .'. Thus 'You be Secretary' is a (pretty firmly) suggested course of action, inviting agreement. The distinction between *caught* and *escaped* is, as far as recording is concerned, purely mechanical. A *caught proposal* is one that is immediately followed by a reaction, no matter what the verbal reaction may be. Even if it is violent disagreement, at least the proposal has not been wasted on the empty air. A proposal is classed as *escaped* when the next behaviour bears no relation at all to it, and indeed it is as if the proposal had never been made. Although relatively crude, this distinction gives interesting insights into, for example, the skills of a group or the influentiality of individuals.

Building This appears to be a very significant behaviour and its incidence bears a close relationship to successful interactions in many situations. A *build* is recorded when someone takes up a proposal and adds something to it that increases its value by way of completeness. So, for example, taking a proposal like 'Let's ring Accounts and get the facts' and turning it into 'Let *me* ring Bill Stephens *right away* and find out (a) the budget totals, (b) current expenditure rates and (c) the forecast 72/73 deficit' makes the original idea sharper and more do-able. Similarly the considerable skill of putting ideas together so that the sum of them is much increased in value ranks as *building*.

Offering (uninvited) explanations, reasons and difficulties This category covers instances where someone brings up, of his own volition, some evidence of opinion or fact that he foresees will cause trouble. A common instance is the group member who draws attention to the fact that time is slipping away, without offering or seeking a suggestion as to what should be done about this state. Recently a group was brought to a complete and depressed halt when just about to go into action on a task that involved going into the open air. One member sombrely announced 'It's started raining – hard.' The resulting delay, confusion, discussion and general demotivation might have been avoided had he said 'Let's rustle up some macs and umbrellas' and thus presented an action-oriented, graspable proposal.

Multi-speak This is an easy one to recognise and provides one of the more obvious yardsticks of performance. When a group is producing 35 per cent of all its behaviour in this category and averaging over 25 per cent in a series of tasks, it is possible to make some immediate inference about listening.

These behavioural categories and the others shown in FIGURE 10 form the basis of a behaviour analysis commonly used in ICL – a behaviour analysis that has been developed over a period of time. As people concerned with the learning process for others, we have also set about the task of learning for ourselves from our own experience and ploughing back the results of that experience in the form of developing and improving practices. Since the original BA was devised in early 1969, surveys – described and discussed in the previous chapter – have subvened to enable us to relate the behaviour we seek to identify to the work environment for which the training programme is designed. Similarly, carefully structured interviews with intending delegates and their managers have provided modifying inputs. A current example is a course we are running mainly for centrally-based personnel staff who need to exercise particular skills in the areas of persuading, influencing and advising people over whom they have no executive authority. In this instance our BA categories reflect a weighting towards behaviours appropriate to such situations. We shall use one category by way of example

Testing the level of understanding or agreement is a development of a previous category which was called *testing understanding*. This latter behaviour as distinct from asking direct questions of clarification, covered statements like 'To be sure we know what we're talking about, let me repeat what I think you're saying in my own words.' Now, although *testing understanding* had emerged in a survey as of some significance in relation to managerial effectiveness, since it hardly ever occurred in the training situation there was no point in including it when there was a queue of other behaviours wanting to find a place on a sheet that, alas, has to have tight limits if the trainer is to have a chance of keeping his observations and recording with the pace of the group. It now reappears in developed form in the light of a set of specific training needs.

It would be possible to write at very much greater length of the trials, errors, and success we have had in constructing and developing behaviour analysis categories and formats. The fundamental issue at stake is, however, that the behavioural data collected must be relevant and comprehensible to course members and must be perceived as such by them. Hence the message to any potential behaviour analyst reader must be to identify what is relevant behaviour in his own field and then to use whatever guidelines these paragraphs may provide.

BEHAVIOUR ANALYSIS DEVELOPMENT IN BOAC

The behaviour analysis shown in FIGURE 11 is being used in BOAC at the time of writing. It is used not only within the context of courses but also in job situations, where it is being developed to assist training needs analysis. Before taking a closer look at a few of the categories a brief word about the way in which they are obviously paired – such as with

11 behaviour analysis BOAC

DATE: 24.2.71 OBSERVER: SBT
GROUP: C TASK: 14

NAME	Jean	Mike	John	Mark	Peter	Jim				T O T A L
SUPPORTING	⊔⊔⊤ III	⊔⊔⊤ ⊔⊔⊤ ⊔⊔⊤ II	II	IIII	IIII	⊔⊔⊤				
DISAGREEING		⊔⊔⊤ III	II	I	I	IIII				
BUILDING		⊔⊔⊤ III	III	IIII	IIII	⊔⊔⊤ I				
CRITICISING		II			II	I				
BRINGING IN	IIII	⊔⊔⊤ III				⊔⊔⊤				
SHUTTING OUT	II	IIII	II	III	II	II				
INNOVATING		III				II				
SOLIDIFYING	III	II	I	III		⊔⊔⊤ I				
ADMITTING DIFFICULTY		II	I			I				
DEFENDING/ ATTACKING		II								
GIVING INFORMATION	⊔⊔⊤ ⊔⊔⊤ II	⊔⊔⊤ ⊔⊔⊤ ⊔⊔⊤ ⊔⊔⊤ ⊔⊔⊤ ⊔⊔⊤ I	⊔⊔⊤ ⊔⊔⊤ ⊔⊔⊤ II	⊔⊔⊤ ⊔⊔⊤ IIII	⊔⊔⊤ ⊔⊔⊤ ⊔⊔⊤ III	⊔⊔⊤ ⊔⊔⊤ ⊔⊔⊤ ⊔⊔⊤ ⊔⊔⊤ I				
SEEKING INFORMATION	⊔⊔⊤ II	⊔⊔⊤ ⊔⊔⊤ ⊔⊔⊤ ⊔⊔⊤ ⊔⊔⊤ ⊔⊔⊤ I	I	⊔⊔⊤ ⊔⊔⊤ I	II	⊔⊔⊤ II				
OTHER										

admitting difficulty and *defending/attacking, building* and *criticising*. This development, which owes something to the results and implications of a survey conducted in BOAC, is an attempt to provide the supervisor with a conceptual framework to help him internalise behavioural feedback. This framework, linking as it does certain categories of behaviour to recognisable supervisory styles, helps the supervisor to think and plan in terms of behavioural strategies; and appears to accelerate awareness of the fact that behavioural strategies are situationally dependent. The feedback implications of this approach are discussed in the next chapter.

That said, let us now look more closely at the way in which the behaviour analysis system has been developed in BOAC since early 1969. We can begin by examining the fate of some of the categories that featured in the original BA.

In successive courses this BA was modified progressively both in content and in processing to provide a more effective instrument for measuring group behaviour. Analysis of data collected resulted in changes such as

Clarifying This category was re-examined, as it had shown very little change in overall incidence during each course. However, for certain individuals it seemed to be an important behaviour category, increasing in frequency moderately throughout the course and associated with building behaviour. It seemed likely that the clarifying category measured two primary areas

● an individual giving other group members clarification of his own views

● an individual asking other group members to clarify their views

It was therefore decided to divide clarifying behaviour into the double category of *seeking clarification* and *giving clarification*, so that any differences between the two areas could be examined. The results showed that, although the two kinds of clarification were typically associated – having an average correlation of $+0.4$ – there were some quite important differences. *Giving clarification* was significantly associated with disagreeing – average correlation $+0.55$ – while *seeking clarification* was not – averaged correlation $+0.1$. Moreover, although *seeking clarification* increased a little as the course progressed – average correlation against time of 0.3, *giving clarification* was relatively unaffected by time – average correlation 0.1 – and showed large and random variations between groups and between sessions.

It therefore appeared that *giving clarification* was a behaviour which occurred in a rather haphazard manner, particularly in response to disagreement within the group. Further work with video tape showed that *giving clarification* was being used as a residual category for almost any exchange of information between group members. As this could be analysed much more effectively by a purpose built behaviour analysis system which categorised classes of exchanged information, it was decided to abandon the *giving clarification* category and to retain *seeking clarification* for the time being.

Confusing This category was taken out of the BA because it was the least frequently used category. It was originally included as the opposite of *clarifying* but because of its very low incidence it was not providing much useful or reliable information.

Just as categories disappear so others are introduced – here are two examples

Talking over It was observed that in the early stages of a group's interactions there tended to be a great deal of interruption, with several individuals often talking simultaneously over the top of each other's contributions. This made the process of recording a behaviour analysis very much more difficult. It seemed that, as this level of interruption was characteristic of the relatively early stages in a group's life, it might in itself provide a useful measure of group progress. We therefore introduced a behaviour analysis category of *talking over*, which recorded interruptions and simultaneous contributions. We found that this category decreased very significantly, especially during the first half of the course, showing an overall average correlation against time of − 0.7.

This category was subsequently developed into *shutting out*, a category that appears on the BA shown in FIGURE 11. *Shutting out* is a behaviour which excludes, or attempts to exclude, other group members. Examples are 'Shut up Fred.', 'Let's put it to the vote without any more discussion.', 'Don't ask questions now.'. Behaviours previously categorised under *talking over* (which resembles ICL's *multi-speak*) are now included under *shutting out*.

Defending/attacking This behaviour category is defined as one which defends or strengthens an individual's own contribution against others, or attacks other people and their contributors. Examples are; 'Well I'm sure I'm right, even if you don't agree.' 'You're trying to get at me!' Defending somebody else or their contribution would not be included under this category.

Our earlier experiments with video tape started with separate categories of *defending behaviour* and *attacking behaviour*. However, there was such a high correlation between them – above $+0.85$ – that they both seemed to be part of a larger, aggressive behaviour syndrome for which no single, readily-understood word exists in the English language. The average correlation of this composite category against time was -0.4. Characteristically, changes in the frequency of this category tend to occur relatively late in the course, usually following feedback – the subject of the next chapter.

We hope these few examples help to give some insight into the process of developing a behaviour analysis system. The BA itself has allowed us to question some of the major assumptions common to most forms of task centred training (thus the disappearance of *systematic behaviour* from the original BA!) and has provided a rational and objective basis for removing noise from the system. At the same time, training considerations and survey findings have caused us to revise the BA categories – making them more intelligible to course members and easier for trainers to use.

This gives the cue to move on and consider how the trainers in ICL and BOAC tackle the task of completing behaviour analyses. What goes on in the course room? How are the trainers trained? What are the reactions of supervisors and managers involved? Let us now look at the ICL and BOAC answers to these and other questions.

HOW THE DATA IS COLLECTED IN ICL

The trainer is present at all times during group work – unless of course he proves sufficiently clumsy in his own

behaviour that he is thrown out by them! Early on – and
quickly – he must learn the names of the group members
and to recognise them by sight and more important, through
their voices. He has to station himself in such a way that,
without intruding or becoming a focus of the group's attention he can see and hear as much as possible of what is
going on. His job then, as a collector of behavioural data,
is to observe, categorise and record as much as he possibly
can. (He has other tasks and indeed earns much of his
recognition by the group in his role of process consultant,
helping them to identify, examine and cope with their own
experience in the situation. These facets of the trainer's role
are discussed at length in the next chapter.)

The end product of his observation is tally marks on a
behaviour analysis sheet, indicating the incidence of the
behaviours of the group and of individuals. FIGURE 10 is an
example of a completed BA sheet. Here is an example of
conversation, taken from a training situation, where the
behaviour category that the trainer would score in the way
shown in FIGURE 10 is noted against each contribution.

A	Who do we want for chairman this time? *Seeking suggestions*
B	I think you should be. *Proposal*
C	Yes I agree. *Supporting*
D	But I thought that we were going to rotate chairmanship round the table. Isn't that so? *Seeking clarification*
E	Look! We have got no time to argue about this. Who agrees it should be A? *Seeking confirmation*
C, E, F	Agreed. *Supporting*
A	Well then, what about our task. Can anyone suggest a definition? *Seeking suggestions*
D	This is going to be a tough one . . . we're going to be pushed for time . . . *Difficulty stating*
B	Rubbish! *Disagreeing, criticising*
A to D	Why do you say that? *Seeking clarification*
D	Well, you know – I suppose it's . . . actually it reminds me of one we did on Monday. Now that was tricky. They often are of course. Still I'm

learning a lot . . . I'm sure we all are . . . *Un-structured contribution*

B, C, E, F I suggest we . . .
Why don't we . . .
Oh for heaven's sake . . . } *Multi-speak*
He's off again . . .

Each contribution made by course members is categorised by its constituent parts. Thus in our extract of discussion above what D says

'But I thought we were going to rotate chairmanship around the table. Isn't that so?'

is recorded as a *seeking of clarification*. Longer contributions are best analysed into more than one behaviour category however. For example, a contribution like this

'Yes I agree with that entirely. It seems to me that we have two suggestions either of which would be acceptable. I think that we should choose between these two, rather than spending a lot more time thinking up other alternatives'

would be recorded as *supporting, other behaviour* (providing explanation in response to request), and *proposing* (either caught or escaped depending on the next thing to happen). There are of course lots of variations on this theme. Not only can the behaviour categories themselves vary depending on the purposes of the occasion, but also the method of categorisation itself. For example, an alternative approach which we have used is to categorise a contribution by giving special attention to its last constituent part. The rationale for this is that the most influential part of a contribution – influential that is in terms of its effects upon the perceptions, and therefore behavioural reactions, of other people – is perhaps its tail-piece. So, for example, we can see that if someone says

'No I'm sorry I can't go along with that because it simply isn't realistic to assume that Bill can get the figures distributed to everyone by then'

the listeners will conclude that the speaker is raising an objection of some kind and be moved to respond accordingly. If, however, our imaginary speaker finishes what he was saying with

'So I suggest that we get an estimate from Bill of how long it will take, and then agree the actual target date' this is likely to be perceived by the listeners as a proposal, or even as a bit of building on whatever the original suggestion might have been, and the resultant reactions may be quite different.

The precise method of categorisation can, therefore, vary depending on the purposes

The precise method of categorisation can, therefore, vary depending on the purposes. This form of behaviour analysis cannot distinguish the duration of behaviour. A straight 'I disagree' will be indistinguishable in the record from a 20 second contribution that boils down to just the same thing. Equally it does not permit analysis of the sequencing of behaviours. These two methods of categorising behaviour are without doubt well worth striving for and a later chapter will discuss them as planned developments. Nevertheless, whatever the method of categorisation, what matters is that the information which is assembled is valid. Invalid data doesn't just jeopardise, but actually destroys the trainers' primary means of controlling the learning situation.

What of the instrument's and the trainers' reliability? Training staff in the coaching role operate within a total of some three dozen standards of performance, of which four relate specifically to behaviour analysing. We conduct frequent monitoring of trainers' performance in behaviour analysis, both in the live course situations and in off-course situations using our own meetings, tapes and video material. Inter-coach correlations very rarely emerge at less than the 0.8 level and often range up to the 0.9 area. These correlations have been achieved between all our training staff and periodic samples are equally reassuring.

An hour-long session produces anything from 280 to 420 behaviours

Finally there is the sheer volume of the data. An hour-long session produces anything from 280 to 420 behaviours on record for an eight member group. On a 24-man course the total bank by the end of the week is usually in the range 7 860 to 12 390 items, while for individuals the quantity will range from 300 to 2 500; the ratio between highest and lowest rates obviously being greater for individuals than for whole courses.

This sheer volume of data that can be accessed by individuals or groups, that can be analysed over time, that is broken down into well-defined classifications and that is related, through survey and other pre-course activities, to the realities of delegates' managerial situations is hard to treat lightly and impossible to ignore.

HOW THE DATA IS COLLECTED IN BOAC

At the beginning of our courses we allocate a coach (ie an observer) to each group and he stays constantly with them until groups are remixed. Although they are given the name coach for historical reasons, observers do not intervene or even answer questions substantively. Any participation by the observer courts disaster. Not only does the impartiality and real role of the coach become suspect, but the behaviour analysis recording runs the risk of being tarred by the same brush.

When we first began using the behaviour analysis system there was some trepidation over the group members' likely reaction to the presence of an observer completing a behaviour analysis. There are frequent mentions of these problems – observer effects – in the literature, and we thought these might be attenuated as we were dealing with a supervisory rather than managerial population. Such fears were in fact unfounded.

We have identified a variety of factors – mostly planned – which we feel are responsible for the absence of adverse reactions. The almost continuous presence of an observer in the group ensures that supervisors on a BOAC course really get used to having an observer present – and quite quickly come to view him as part of the scenery. Sample recording cannot meet this requirement. Further, the fact that all observers are staff members of BOAC, all actively involved in training, makes the behaviour recording a more acceptable activity. Many reported studies have problems of observer effect merely because the observer was perceived as an outsider – even as a research person! Finally we are completely open about the behaviour analysis system and the precise function of the observer right from the start of the course. The actual observation sheets are freely available and as part of the preliminary sessions leading up to the first feedback session course members are told about the categories of behaviour used, and the behaviour classification related to meaningful on-the-job examples.

The fact that all observers are staff members of BOAC makes the behaviour recording a more acceptable activity

Turning now to the nuts and bolts issue of the precise
method of categorisation used by observers in BOAC, you
will see from this example that we use a similar method to
that employed by ICL, except that in BOAC contributions
may be recorded occasionally under more than one behaviour category. Here is a typical example of how we use
behaviour categories

Harry 'Any ideas Bill?' *Bringing in*
Bill 'Well I think the best way to tackle it, would be
to divide the work between the four of us.' *Innovating*
Harry 'Yes, that's a good idea.' *Supporting*. 'John and I
could do the costing bit between us, and then . . .'
Building
John (**interrupting him**) 'Speak for yourself mate!'
Shutting-out, disagreeing. 'You've had me doing costings
work all this week, while you've been taking it easy.'
Criticising
Harry 'Nonsense! I've done more than my fair share'
defending/attacking. 'Anyway I suggested we did it
together this time.' *Solidifying*
John 'So you did' *Supporting*. 'Sorry, I jumped to
conclusions again.' *Admitting difficulty*

An example of a completed BOAC behaviour analysis is
shown in FIGURE 11.
The BA used in this way can only provide us with data about
totals of behaviour categories for each member of the group.
Other behavioural data is lost using this system.
What exactly is lost? Traditionally people using behaviour
analysis techniques have collected more information than
we collect. Not only do they record who originated a
particular behaviour, but also to whom it is directed. To
record in such detail poses practical problems which are
difficult to solve. For one thing, it places a much greater
load on the observer. In group situations with as many as
eight people the identification of even the contributor, much
less the receiver, of a communication becomes a difficult
task. Obtaining reliability between observers naturally
becomes more difficult to obtain. It is not always clear who
are the active recipients of any interactive exchange and
who are merely passive listeners.

A more significant loss in the present system is the sequence of behaviour made by individuals and particularly their response to specific behaviours of others. While many analyses employ procedures which obtain data on such a contribution-by-contribution or sequencing basis, the data produced has rarely been used fully. This stems from the fact that the data processing and statistical load is very considerable.

In our own activities we are most concerned, in the short term, with combinations of behaviour in particular contributions, rather than with the strategies, sequences or responses within a series of contributions. We have considerable evidence, both from our own research and from an earlier on-the-job behaviour analysis in BEA, that there is little relationship between the simple content of a contribution or interactive episode and its total duration. This is why we are presently concerned with total frequency rather than duration.

In future behaviour analysis work on-the-job in BOAC and as well as in group situations we will continue to rely on frequency totals of behaviour, while sequence analysis will be carried out.

TRAINING THE TRAINERS

So far we have discussed the two important issues of trainee reactions to data collection, and the method of categorising behaviour. Let us conclude by examining the vital question of observer reliability. This fundamental issue has more than the usual significance for us because it is our policy and practice in BOAC, as in ICL, to draw upon our own training staff to act as coaches.

The activity of introducing new observers into courses is naturally closely related to the whole question of observer reliability. The model of training shown in FIGURE 12 has evolved over some time and has only recently become formalised to meet the needs for reliable measurements and the lower previous experience of people who are now trained up to be observers. The problem is common to both companies and ICL has also developed detailed observer training models which are adapted to the specific needs of its training systems. All newcomers to the coaching

113 Michael J Colbert
Michael Morris
Stephen Tribe

The first priority of new trainers is to become proficient at recording behaviour role have as a first priority the requirement to become proficient at recording behaviour – and the model illustrates only how this requirement is tackled. It does not take account of other significant skills, notably the ability to feed back behavioural data to groups.

Depending on the past experience of new observers, an early decision is made on whether they should attend an external interactive skills course. The factors which would mediate against the need to attend a course of this sort would be the individual's knowledge of behavioural science, previous involvement in skills training and a judgment on the appropriateness for this person of a sensitising experience. We have not used our own courses for this purpose.

While we consider that external courses do suffer from some important methodological defects already outlined in this series, we think that new observers gain more than the usual attendee. They become aware of the difficulties faced by coaches when coaches make themselves vulnerable by intervening and by feeding back only unquantified and undefendable judgments, even though these may represent years of acquired knowledge of similar situations. The drawbacks of a lack of real course objectives and the chance composition of groups usually also become apparent – certainly in retrospect when they have been involved in our own courses.

Preliminary training within BOAC involves a week's attendance at a course where they are able to read up the history of interactive skills training to date, and learn the behaviour categories, and their definitions, in current use. While not active in these, they are present in the operations room where they can not only assist in some clerical tasks but become involved in all activity other than the coaches' role.

The more systematic training in behaviour analysis is very adaptable as far as the timetable of events. For some coaches it may be necessary, due to other demands on his or her time, for each step illustrated to be taken at weekly intervals. There is a great deal to be said for keeping the time between the stages in the sequence as short as practicable.

The first stage beyond the learning of behaviour definitions

12 behaviour analysis training in BOAC

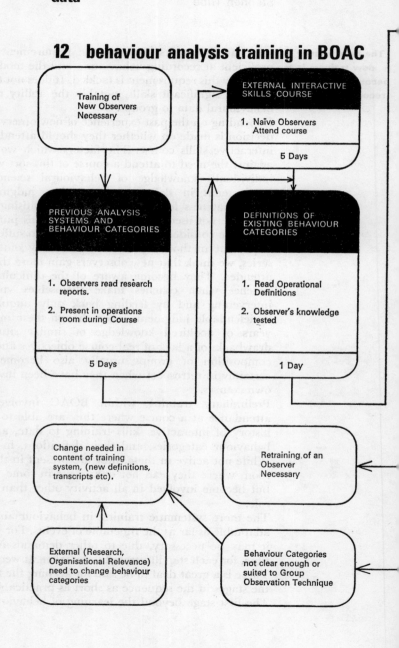

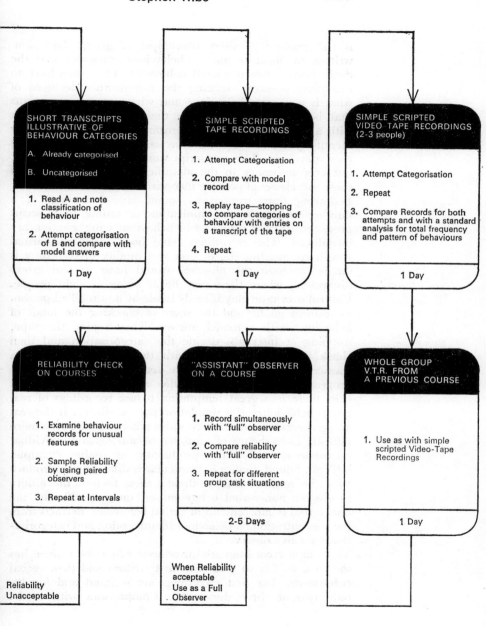

is the reading of short transcripts of group discussion, written to illustrate all the behaviour categories and the distinctions between related behaviour. They then have to categorise passages – making the two distinct decisions of what is a discrete behaviour and what category represents that behaviour – and compare their categorised transcript with a model answer. With assistance they then separately identify problems of behaviour *unit* and behaviour *content* they may have. This transcript work is essentially leisurely, but very necessary to the identification and correction of these two classes of possible inconsistency in later analyses.

Following from transcripts, sound tape recordings of a number of people communicating according to a script produced to raise problems of behaviour categorisation are introduced. The recordings have been made at normal speech speeds, but the diction and quality of recording is far better than the observer would have in real group discussions, where there may be as many as eight people. Control over tape play is easily made by an unskilled person, so trainees go beyond the stage of checking the totals of behaviour with a model answer. They replay the tape, stopping at intervals, decide the categorisation and then check for its co-incidence with the model answer in a transcript of the tape. We are readily able to assess the progress of coaches. When video recording and playback exist there is a great temptation to use recordings of real group behaviours as a simulation par excellence. If the real group observations are tricky, video recordings are even more difficult. Even the use of a number of cameras and individual microphones makes the production of usable examples difficult. Sound quality in particular is difficult to reproduce with the original clarity. Besides these factors, the ability to observe non-verbal behaviour or, more specifically, the non-verbal reinforcements of verbal behaviour, detracts from the concentration on behaviour identification and categorisation for naïve observers.

Video tape recordings are introduced when the trainee has shown a facility to deal with first written and then verbal behaviours. The first recordings are scripted and involve only two or three discussants. Comparisons with model answers are made as in the previous stages. Finally video tape recordings are introduced to prepare the trainee for the situation on courses. We do not expect these observers to achieve the reliability levels which are obtained on courses. In courses there is some considerable time for the observer to get to know and recognise the verbal contribution of each member of the group he is coaching.

The time necessary for the final stage in the learning process, that is obtaining high reliability compared with a full coach on a course, varies considerably. We have not found it necessary as yet to continue an observer's assistant role beyond a week.

The achievement of a successful reliability coefficient for a couple of sessions is not the end of the story. As in ICL coaches are subject to periodic checks by simultaneous recording – as many coaches as possible for a particular session. This may have two possible outcomes. Either some coaches may need retraining or, in certain circumstances, changes in behaviour categories or definitions may be necessary. The materials (transcripts, tape examples) used in the training schemes are subject to some revision when change in behaviour categories are made due to this reason or because of an external requirement.

CONCLUSION

This is how ICL and BOAC trainers collect behavioural data. As has been hinted at here and there, other behaviour analyses are used for diagnostic, development and other purposes. Like behaviour itself, behaviour analyses are situationally dependent! No one behaviour analysis can cope with all the data collection needs of the trainer.

None of us involved in the development of this training believes, or would want anyone else to believe, that we are, in any sense, quantifying the unquantifiable. But we are confident that the data we collect, with all its limitations, provides us with more useful raw material than would otherwise be available.

Should it all seem too formidable a task then we ask you to remember our opening statement – **WHAT YOU CANNOT MEASURE YOU CANNOT CONTROL.** ✳

chapter 5

ÎNTERACTÎVE SKÎLLS

feeding back
behavioural data

PETER HONEY
RAY FIELDS ICL
DEREK HINSON BOAC

**The ultimate purpose in acquiring knowledge
is to do something with it; to use it in some way.
The previous chapter showed how knowledge
about interpersonal behaviour can be gathered
up by an observer. This chapter takes the story
two stages further by showing how the data is
processed, and in particular, by describing the
use to which it is put after it has been analysed.
Our current concern, therefore, is with how
the data about interpersonal behaviour which
has been assembled by the process of
behaviour analysis is fed back to participating
managers during their training experience.**

119 Peter Honey
Ray Fields
Derek Hinson

FEEDBACK IS A WELL-RECOGNISED INGREDIENT OF THE learning process. It has been shown time and time again to be a vital component, since feedback provides information for corrective action. This seems true both in the realm of motor skills and in social or interactive skills. A blindfolded man can't drive a car very successfully because he has been deprived of his main source of feedback which, in that situation, is visual. Similarly an insensitive manager cannot adjust his behaviour in an interactive situation unless he realises that it is inappropriate in some way. For example, he may be unintentionally annoying his colleagues. He comes to realise that this is so by collecting feedback information from the behaviour of the other people. He may notice that they start to participate less, or that they keep looking at the clock or that they seem defensive or aggressive and, if all else fails, he may notice it when someone actually tells him that he is annoying them!

Actually it is quite interesting to reflect on the role that feedback plays in procedures and practices which are designed to bring about change in human behaviour. Take, for example, appraisal systems which come in many different shapes and sizes, of course, but which are all based on the assumption that the minimum that a man requires in order to be willing and able to improve his job performance is

● information about what is expected of him
objectives, standards etc

● information about how his performance matches up to this expectation   *feedback*

The appraisal process assumes that knowledge of results is a must and that, if people don't get performance feedback from some external source, then they fall to assessing their own performance – using their own standards. This sort of self-stimulation can result in dreadful misunderstandings when, for example, the performer eventually receives feedback information which is greatly at variance with that which he has been giving himself. Consider also the role of feedback in process consultation and the various strategies for organisation development. Feeding back non-evaluative, diagnostic data to the people in the organisation who can take action is seen to be far more influential a process, from the change agent's point of view, than either the gathering of the data or the implementation of eventual action based upon the data. It wouldn't be difficult to go on generating examples to show that feedback is an important ingredient in the process of learning, but perhaps it isn't necessary when writing for a target population of trainers.

Feedback is a vital ingredient in any process of learning

However, it is one thing to know that feedback is a vital ingredient in any process of learning and quite another to do something positive about it. Every trainer has lots of feedback possibilities to choose from. He can design learning situations in which the learners collect feedback from each other, collect feedback from the trainer, collect feedback from the results they achieve during training, or any blend of these. He has a choice between evaluative or non-evaluative feedback and can decide the extent to which feedback will be specific or open to processes of induction.

Feedback strategies need to be planned quite consciously and deliberately

We find in our work that feedback strategies need to be planned quite consciously and deliberately. The way in which the trainer intervenes, for example, makes a tremendous difference to the reactions of the learners. Various investigations have shown just how powerful a factor the trainer's behaviour can be. We ourselves have discovered that if a trainer, sitting in as a group observer, nods and smiles at certain stages in the group's work, and shakes his head and frowns at others, this alone helps to shape and influence what the group does and doesn't do. This is reminiscent of all those experiments into the effects of an interviewer's behaviour on the performance of an interviewee. For the first ten minutes the interviewer conducts a relaxed, non-directive interview; for the second ten minutes he systematically rewards certain types of behaviour on the part of the interviewee. For example, every time the interviewee offers an opinion, the interviewer smiles, agrees, looks him in the eye and makes other approving gestures and noises. For the third ten minutes the interviewer responds negatively to opinions by disagreeing and doing disapproving things, like strumming his fingers or looking at his watch. The interviewee increases the frequency of giving opinions in the second period, and decreases it in the third period.

Bearing all this in mind, we find that the trainer's interventions in the sort of learning-by-doing situations that we are concerned with in interactive skills training need to vary, depending on all sorts of circumstances of course, but not to drift too far from this sort of maxim

● what the trainer says needs to be comprehensible by the learners and needs to be perceived by them as relevant

● what the trainer says needs to be as non-evaluative as possible and phrased in such a way as to maximise the participation of the learners: questions are a good device, since they call for a response

● if the trainer is in doubt about the appropriateness of what he wants to say, then it is best to say nothing – it is surprising how many times a member of the group will say what you were going to say for you!

If all this sounds like a recipe for sitting quietly and never giving feedback, then it shouldn't, because **our work is based upon the belief that it is unrealistic to assume that people will collect either enough and/or valid and/or reliable information when left to their own devices.** This seems to be a particularly important conclusion in the field of social or interpersonal behaviour. You can't learn by your own mistakes unless you recognise a mistake as a mistake. In this grey, organic area of social intercourse, what constitutes a mistake and what a success in any given situation is very much a matter for individual judgment and opinion.

For all these reasons it seems sensible to feed back behavioural data from a third party, and this chapter describes the way this is done in BOAC and in ICL. But first a word about how the behaviour analysis data is knocked into a usefully digestible form. When a course is run in BOAC and in ICL, an operations room is set up. It is manned throughout the course by a behavioural scientist, whose job it is to process the data and to give interpretative help to the trainers and/or course members. (Chapter 7 will show how you can cope without such a person.)

HOW THE DATA IS PROCESSED IN BOAC

In BOAC the trainers return their completed behaviour analysis forms to the operations room at the end of each group activity, which usually last from 45 to 75 minutes. For the most part we have processed the raw data manually, using only a programmable desk calculator, although procedures for making use of computer facilities have been developed and tested. Computer processing will be carried out on all courses shortly, since with printouts a greater amount of information can be presented more readily to members. More importantly, perhaps, the faster processing will provide us with the option of giving feedback more frequently where it is judged useful to do this.

Under the manual system, however, we first total the tally marks on the forms down the columns to give individually-oriented data and across the rows to give group-oriented data. We keep a data record sheet for every course member and the totals recorded for every behaviour category per session are transferred to this sheet – FIGURE 13. Thus throughout the course, we have available on one document

13 BOAC - individual data record sheet

COURSE MEMBER : JOHN W

Session Number	1	2	3	4	5	6	7	1-7 Total	1-7 %
Category									
Supporting	1	1	1	0	3	1	5	12	3.9
Disagreeing	4	1	4	6	1	4	10	30	9.6
Building	0	0	1	1	0	0	7	9	2.9
Criticising	3	0	3	6	1	0	4	17	5.5
Bringing in	3	1	2	4	2	2	1	15	4.8
Shutting out	1	0	0	3	0	0	1	5	1.6
Innovating	5	0	13	6	5	8	3	40	12.8
Solidifying	20	0	6	12	7	3	2	50	16.0
Admitting Difficulties	2	0	1	2	0	0	2	7	2.2
Defending/Attacking	3	0	1	9	1	4	2	20	6.4
Giving Information	5	4	10	7	8	10	27	71	22.8
Seeking Information	8	1	4	4	3	1	5	26	8.3
Other Behaviours	0	3	3	1	1	2	0	10	3.2
TOTAL	55	11	49	61	32	35	69	312	100%

an up-to-date record for each course member. These figures are totalled periodically, usually at the end of each day, and are calculated in percentage terms. This makes it easier for both the trainers and course members to see the pattern emerging and changes that are taking place throughout the course.

At the end of each training session course members complete a brief self-rating questionnaire showing how they feel about such things as involvement and group atmosphere. As with the ICL session assessments described later, these ratings are given a score and recorded on the individual record sheets. We have, therefore, in the operations room a running account of the behaviour patterns and perceptions of each individual, which is under continuous study by the behavioural scientist and the trainers.

In the earlier stages of development the group oriented behavioural data was also recorded in percentage terms for each session. The results were displayed in the operations room in the form of a histogram with the behaviour categories shown in different colours. While these group charts were a very effective visual aid in initially drawing the attention of course members to the pattern of behaviours in a group and in illustrating the changing pattern, they had disadvantages. They tended, for example, to focus too much attention on group, and inter-group, performance as opposed to individual performance, which is more important to us and the course members. For this and other reasons, group data is no longer displayed, although we do make use of normative group data for comparative purposes in feedback sessions.

To help the trainers in these sessions another document is prepared providing on one sheet a summary of the behavioural data for a given period for all members of a group. This is illustrated in FIGURE 14, which gives both raw scores and percentage figures for a six member group. Thus in Tasks 16-22 Alan had recorded 57 SUPPORTING contributions, and these represented 14.3 per cent of his total contributions for that period. We have in practice added coloured symbols to these summary sheets to highlight particular categories – those increasing or decreasing

14 data summary BOAC

Date: 09/12/70   Observer: JDH

Group: 2   Tasks: 16-22

NAME	ALAN	JEFF	TONY	MIKE	ANNE	PETER	TOTAL GROUP
SUPPORTING	14·3 / 57	13·8 / 54	13·5 / 36	20·5 / 36	13·6 / 42	12·4 / 53	14·1 / 278
DISAGREEING	3·8 / 15	4·9 / 19	1·9 / 5	5·1 / 9	3·2 / 10	4·0 / 17	3·8 / 75
BUILDING	6·3 / 25	6·6 / 26	9·0 / 24	5·1 / 9	5·2 / 16	9·8 / 42	7·2 / 142
CRITICISING	1·0 / 4	1·0 / 4	1·1 / 3	0 / 0	1·0 / 3	1·4 / 6	1·0 / 20
BRINGING IN	8·5 / 34	11·8 / 46	5·3 / 14	6·8 / 12	10·7 / 33	4·9 / 21	8·1 / 160
SHUTTING OUT	5·3 / 21	4·1 / 16	4·1 / 11	9·1 / 16	4·2 / 13	4·9 / 21	5·0 / 98
INNOVATING	2·0 / 8	3·3 / 13	3·8 / 10	1·1 / 2	3·6 / 11	3·3 / 14	2·9 / 58
SOLIDIFYING	16·5 / 66	16·1 / 63	19·2 / 51	9·1 / 16	12·0 / 37	15·4 / 66	15·2 / 299
ADMITTING DIFFICULTY	2·3 / 9	1·0 / 4	0·8 / 2	1·1 / 2	0·3 / 1	0·0 / 1	0·9 / 18
DEFENDING/ATTACKING	3·5 / 14	5·1 / 20	1·9 / 5	2·3 / 4	4·9 / 15	4·9 / 21	4·0 / 79
GIVING INFORMATION	24·1 / 96	18·9 / 74	30·5 / 81	29·5 / 52	24·7 / 76	29·7 / 127	25·7 / 506
SEEKING INFORMATION	12·5 / 50	13·3 / 52	9·0 / 24	10·2 / 18	16·6 / 51	9·3 / 40	11·9 / 235
TOTAL	100 / 399	100 / 391	100 / 266	100 / 176	100 / 308	100 / 428	100 / 1968

125 Peter Honey
Ray Fields
Derek Hinson

significantly as the course progresses, for example, so that this document provides the trainer with most of the basic reference data he will require for the feedback session.

HOW THE DATA IS PROCESSED IN ICL

In ICL, not surprisingly perhaps, we have used a computer for processing raw data and producing printouts on every course run during the past two years or so. The idea is to get the computer to do our sums for us and to produce printouts, which can be handed straight on to course members – enabling them to extract a profile, not only of their own behaviour, but also that of the group and then to see the links between the two. Inevitably during our development of this work we have tried out quite a few printout formats, some of which have proved more helpful to course members than others. For the purposes of this article, only three of the most frequently-used formats will be described and two of them illustrated (FIGURES 15, 16). The DATA COLLAPSE printout is simply a summary of group and individual behaviour over a period of time. The layout

The printout is seen to be quite lush with fascinating data

takes a few moments to get used to, but once mastered the printout is seen to be quite lush with fascinating data. Not only can any individual course member establish plenty about his own behaviour, but he also has comparative data about the behaviour of his particular group, and, indeed, about the behaviour of his colleagues. So for example, Vall is able to see that, amongst other things, he is the group's top disagreer – his 29 recorded instances of this behaviour represent 35.4 per cent of the group's disagreeing behaviour – and that his own personal percentage is well above the group percentage – his 29 recorded instances of this behaviour represent 10.1 per cent of his own behaviour, which compares with a total group percentage of only 6.1. Vall can also see lots of other things about his own behaviour in relation to others, not least, for example, that he is the group's highest contributor with 287 recorded behaviours, which is 21.3 per cent of the number of recorded behaviours for the group.

On the next two pages FIGURE 15 shows a specimen Data Collapse printout, used in ICL as a record of behaviours.

15 data collapse printout ICL

Indicates tasks covered by this collapse

Individual Group Member

Behaviour category

This category expressed as a % of group's total behaviour

Recorded instances of this behaviour in group

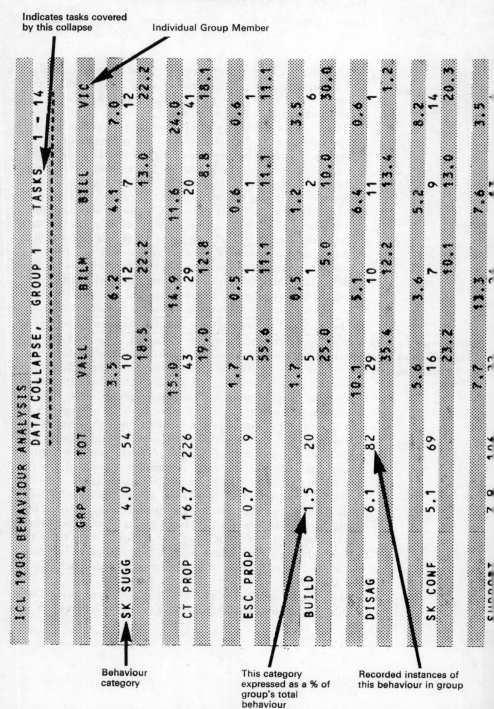

ICL 1900 BEHAVIOUR ANALYSIS
DATA COLLAPSE, GROUP 1   TASKS 1 - 14

	GRP %	TOT	VALL		BILM		BILL		VIC	
SK SUGG	4.0	54	3.5	10	6.2	12	4.1	7	7.0	12
			18.5		22.2		13.0		22.2	
CT PROP	16.7	226	15.9	43	14.9	29	11.6	20	24.0	41
			19.0		12.8		8.8		13.1	
ESC PROP	0.7	9	1.7	5	0.5	1	0.6	1	0.6	1
			55.6		11.1		11.1		11.1	
BUILD	1.5	20	1.7	5	0.5	1	1.2	2	3.5	6
			25.0		5.0		10.0		30.0	
DISAG	6.1	82	10.1	29	5.1	10	6.4	11	0.6	1
			35.4		12.2		13.4		1.2	
SK CONF	5.1	69	5.6	16	3.6	7	5.2	9	8.2	14
			23.2		10.1		13.0		20.3	
			7.7		13.3		7.6		3.5	

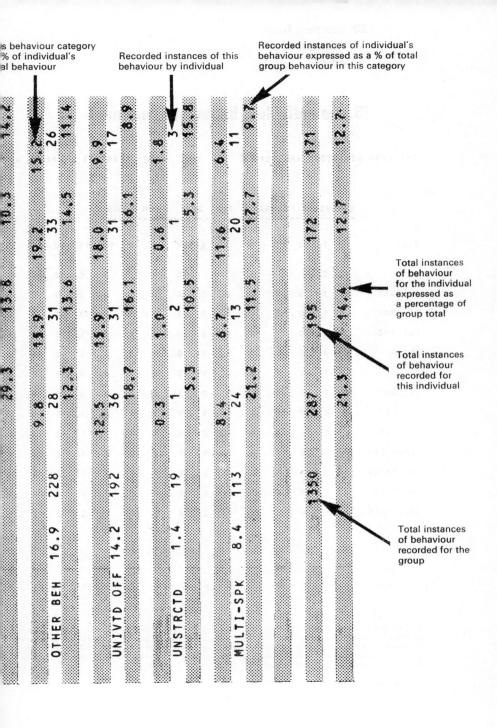

s behaviour category
% of individual's
al behaviour

Recorded instances of this behaviour by individual

Recorded instances of individual's behaviour expressed as a % of total group behaviour in this category

Total instances of behaviour for the individual expressed as a percentage of group total

Total instances of behaviour recorded for this individual

Total instances of behaviour recorded for the group

16 the individual behaviour summary

```
ICL 1900 BEHAVIOUR ANALYSIS                    DATE 11/01/71    PAGE 401
```

BEHAVIOUR SUMMARY FOR BILL FROM GROUP 1

TASK	1	2	3	4	5	6	7	8	9	10	11	12	13	14
	C						C			S	C	S	S	
SK SUGG	3	0	0	0	0	0	4	0	0	0	0	0	0	0
CT PROP·	1	0	1	2	0	0	6	0	3	0	3	1	1	2
ESC PROP	0	0	0	0	0	0	0	0	0	0	1	0	0	0
BUILD	0	1	0	0	0	1	0	0	0	0	0	0	0	0
DISAG	1	0	2	2	2	1	0	0	1	0	0	1	1	0
SK CONF	1	1	1	1	0	0	3	0	2	0	0	0	0	0
SUPPORT	2	0	2	1	0	0	0	1	0	3	1	1	0	2
SK CLAR	2	1	5	1	0	2	4	2	3	1	1	2	0	0
OTHER BEH	3	0	6	3	0	1	9	1	2	1	4	2	0	1
UNIVTD OFF	6	2	4	2	2	1	5	3	1	0	1	2	1	1
UNSTRCTD	1	0	0	0	0	0	0	0	0	0	0	0	0	0
MULTI-SPK	1	0	9	1	0	2	2	1	0	1	2	0	0	1
TOT SUM	21	5	30	13	4	8	33	8	12	6	13	9	3	7

This is really a fair copy of the coach's behavioural analysis sheet for the individual concerned, showing the raw score against the behavioural categories. The scores for each task are listed under the appropriate task number. In the example shown we can see that Bill during task 3 was seen to make 2 disagreements and to seek clarification on 5 occasions. The letter C under task 1 and 7 tells us that Bill was chairman during that session.

129 Peter Honey
Ray Fields
Derek Hinson

The one other printout that course members get feeds back data about how the individual felt about each session at its conclusion. Everyone is asked to spend a few seconds filling in the following form

17 ICL management training session assessment

group	initials	session number

1   To what extent did the group achieve its aims?

					✔	

not at all   completely

2   How valuable do you consider the session was to the group?

				✔		

not at all   completely

3   How far did you agree with what the group did during the session?

	✔					

not at all   completely

4   To what extent did you become personally involved in the success or failure of the group?

					✔	

not at all   completely

The printout simply reminds the course member of his reactions to these four questions, so that he can relate his perceptions of the session with his behaviour during it. The printout does this by giving a score to indicate where the course member put his tick on the seven point scale. The example given would score therefore

question 1   *6*
question 2   *5*
question 3   *2*
question 4   *6*

Of course, there are many other alternative methods of analysing this sort of data, but it is important to remember that the overall purpose in analysing it at all is to put it into a form which is easily comprehensible and useful to the course members who are going to have to take action on the basis of the data. The analysis is thoroughly consumer-oriented, therefore. This limits the elegance of the statistical analysis and also puts pretty severe time limits on analytical work, since, the quicker that information can be fed back to the consumer, the more pertinent and influential that information is.

We now turn our attention exclusively to how the behavioural data is fed back to the participants. Again we shall look first at how it is done in BOAC and then at ICL's feedback practices.

HOW THE DATA IS FED BACK IN BOAC

As described in an earlier chapter, the BOAC course has three recognisable stages. We start with a diagnostic stage when the trainer is primarily concerned with recording behavioural data. Once having explained his role to the group, he makes as few interventions as possible into their activities and normally only at their request. Even then his contribution will usually throw the ball back to the group! During the first two days of a course a sample of several hundred behaviours per person will have been processed and the second stage, that of formal feedback to members, can then take place. The first part of day three is taken up with formal feedback, leaving the remainder of the course for the third stage. During this members are encouraged to try out different modes of behaviour to increase their effectiveness and to monitor their performance by reference to the operations room data and the trainers, assisted by a further formal feedback session on the fifth day.

We can now look more closely at what happens during the second and third stages. We really begin the feedback stage on the second day with an introductory session with all course members present, in which one of the trainers describes the data collection and processing system being used. The behaviour categories are defined and, in experience, very easily understood: an important point since this was one of the criteria for selection of categories mentioned in an earlier article. So course members know what information they will be given, but what will it all mean? How is it to be interpreted? Obviously no *ideal pattern of behaviour* associated with some mythical *ideal effective manager* can be prescribed, there is no stereotype to be imitated. Experience tells any manager that different situations demand different methods of approach or different styles – in reality different strategies and combinations of behaviour. The person who in work manages his relationships with other people most effectively is the one who can recognise the style appropriate to the situation and use the relevant strategy.

In the introductory session, therefore, we go on to draw attention to aspects of data interpretation. For example, while no isolated category of behaviour can be judged appropriate or inappropriate in all situations, there is evidence that a related group of the categories occurs at a relatively higher incidence level in groups that are working together less effectively – namely DISAGREEING; CRITICISING; DEFENDING/ATTACKING; and SHUTTING OUT. In contrast, behaviours characteristic of more effective groups are a higher level of BUILDING; SUPPORTING; ADMITTING DIFFICULTY; and SEEKING INFORMATION.

When considering their own performance data, members are advised to look not only at the level of particular categories, but also at the relationship between categories and the possible implications. These two individuals A and B may be equally high on INNOVATING. A may also be high

The person who in work manages his relationships with other people most effectively is the one who can recognise the style appropriate to the situation and use the relevant strategy

We must ask ourselves what moral justification we have for putting people through an experience powerful enough to change personal aspects of their social interactions

on DISAGREEING: DEFENDING/ATTACKING and low on SUPPORTING: BUILDING. *B* could show the reverse pattern on the latter categories. These patterns would indicate that while both are good ideas men, *B* is likely to be more effective than *A* in situations requiring the co-operation of other people in actually getting new things done.

To help members relate the course activity to job situations, we initiate at this point a discussion on styles of management, introducing a number of styles whose characteristics are readily recognised by members. For example, a participative style is analysed and the high-participative manager – who tends to involve his subordinates in decisions which affect them – is contrasted with the low-participative manager – who keeps decisions to himself and is not concerned with the views of others. The relationship of BRINGING IN and SHUTTING-OUT behaviours to the characteristics of the extremes of this style is brought out. In a similar way other categories of behaviours are associated with other styles – eg ADMITTING DIFFICULTY with an open style.

The introductory session, which has been described at some length, is therefore an important part of the feedback process, since it aims to prepare course members for the critical task of evaluating feedback data and deciding what they should try to do to improve their performance. One other activity which precedes the formal feedback session should be mentioned. This is the discussion between the behavioural scientist and the trainers, in which the former gives guidance on the interpretation of all available data. This is linked to the trainers' view of what has been happening and the advice to be given during the feedback is agreed. It is worth noting that, with growing experience, the trainers have been able increasingly to take the lead in interpreting the data, leaving the researchers' expertise to be concentrated on the more unusual problems.

After this discussion the trainers meet their own groups for the feedback session, which normally takes 1-1½ hours. To give some basis for comparison, we often start by giving the figures for the group as a whole, indicating those categories which are significantly higher or lower than typical group norms. Members are asked to think about the behaviours that have been helping them to achieve their objectives in their various activities, and those that have been holding them back. They usually identify fairly quickly the direction in which certain behaviours need to be changed to achieve a more effective performance.

We then move on to the main part of the feedback, giving each member in turn information about his recorded behaviours and highlighting those which vary greatly from the group norm or which seem to have a particular significance. Members are encouraged to give their own reactions to the information, particularly in terms of which behaviours they think they should try to increase or decrease if they are to make a more effective contribution to the group's objectives. The trainer tries to stimulate this analysis by his questions and where possible develops his advice from points raised by the individual.

In one course, for example, over the first two days Mr T had made more than twice as many contributions as six of the seven other members of his group; had produced many ideas taken up by the group; had shown little support for others' ideas; and was above average in his disagreeing and defending. By posing questions such as *Are you really helping your colleagues by putting in all these ideas and making so many contributions?* and *How do you try to give consideration to the views of other people?* in addition to asking for his general reaction to the information, a discussion on changes that he might try was developed. As a result Mr T decided that he would try to cut down his total contributions, to reduce the amount of disagreeing by first seeking more clarification and information from others, and to give more support to other group members. This formed the central part of the feedback advice for Mr T agreed in the operations room discussion, but in the feedback session itself these conclusions were basically reached by Mr T himself.

During the feedback we encourage all members to contribute to the discussion throughout. The trainer often refers to specific incidents in earlier sessions, prompting members to analyse what happened, so that the effects of various behaviours can be more meaningfully assessed. Thus members

help each other to decide what might be suitable or unsuitable behaviour in given situations, and to begin formulat-
ing some personal objectives for the remainder of the course.
We then move on to the third stage of the course in which
members are trying different ways of doing things and
judging for themselves from their experience whether or
not their new methods are enabling them to work more
effectively with others. They have access at all times to the
operations room so that they can check their behavioural
performance and they can also call on the trainers for
guidance if they wish.

Obviously at this stage the course activities are designed
to provide optimum conditions in which members can
develop their skills. For part of the time, for example,
members work in specially selected new groups. We also
give tasks which help members to translate their objectives
(or should we say good intentions!) formed during the
feedback session and immediately afterwards into rather
more specific plans. One such activity stipulates

*Compare and discuss your individual objectives. Devise ways and
means which you can use within this group to achieve at least some
of these objectives.*

Thus members agree with each other how they will try to
achieve their objectives in a somewhat similar way to the
ICL projects described later. After a further three or four
sessions we would ask members to review their progress and
update their plans.

On the final day of the course we have a second formal
feedback session and this is followed by activities in which
members prepare an initial plan for putting what they have
learned into practice back in their job. One recently-
developed aspect of this feedback is perhaps worth mention-
ing before we move on to describe the ICL process.

On day two after the discussion of management styles,
members complete a questionnaire which asks them, in
respect of five identified styles – PARTICIPATIVE; INNOVATIVE;
SUPPORTIVE; OPEN; and DEVELOPING –

*How do you rate yourself on this style compared with other
managers and supervisors in BOAC?*

135 Peter Honey
Ray Fields
Derek Hinson

The rating is on a five-point scale – very high; high; average; slightly below average; well below average.

On day five each member is given the document, shown as FIGURE 18, on which he is reminded of how he rated himself. In addition, the format shows the number of behaviours recorded by the individual in categories which are associated with characteristics of the five styles. Finally, these scores are compared with the scores for all course members (and in time BOAC norms will be established) and a comparative rating made.

Consequently, in this feedback session, the individual has some information on the validity of his earlier perceptions of his own styles of working with other people and can obtain the views of other group members to check out any major differences in the comparative ratings which he finds difficult to accept. We find that members are able and willing to learn from each other. In fact in one course recently group members rated each other on the styles and exchanged this information in a self-chosen activity immediately before the feedback session.

This final feedback session then allows course members to review changes in their performance during the course, derived from the behaviour analysis records; to question further some of the assumptions they had about their way of working with other people; to get the views about themselves of their fellow course members; and leads them into consideration of some of the implications of all this information which is the input for the subsequent final course activities, planning what they can do to improve their performance on the job.

HOW THE DATA IS FED BACK IN ICL

In ICL we tend towards a two stage, rather than a three stage, course design. The first day and perhaps the morning of the second day are regarded as the diagnostic period, during which behavioural data is being assembled and not fed back. From then on there is at least one feedback session per day and this is always individually-oriented. We used to have a group-oriented feedback stage on our courses, but this has now been replaced with a procedure that

18 BOAC - development of supervisory skills course

Date ....20/11/70....

Name....TONY R....

Group ......1......

YOUR SUPERVISORY MANAGEMENT STYLES

For the 5 types of supervisory management styles shown, the numbers of behaviours you have displayed are:

PARTICIPATIVE	DAY 1/2	DAY 3/4	SUPPORTIVE	DAY 1/2	DAY 3/4	DEVELOPING	DAY 1/2	DAY 3/4	INNOVATIVE	DAY 1/2	DAY 3/4	OPEN	DAY 1/2	DAY 3/4
Bringing in	19	26	Supporting	54	47	Building	23	37	Innovating	15	17	Admitting difficulty	4	8
Shutting out	48	34	Disagreeing	25	15	Criticising	8	14	Solidifying	68	45	Defending/attacking	12	21

Compared with the whole course this relationship is:

	PARTICIPATIVE 1/2	PARTICIPATIVE 3/4	SUPPORTIVE 1/2	SUPPORTIVE 3/4	DEVELOPING 1/2	DEVELOPING 3/4	INNOVATIVE 1/2	INNOVATIVE 3/4	OPEN 1/2	OPEN 3/4
Very high	☐	☐	☐	☐	☐	☐	☐	☐	☐	☐
High	☐	☐	☐	☐	☐	☐	☐	☐	☐	☐
Average	☐	☑	☑	☑	☐	☐	☐	☑	☑	☑
Slightly below average	☑	☐	☐	☐	☑	☑	☑	☐	☐	☐
Well below average	☐	☐	☐	☐	☐	☐	☐	☐	☐	☐

You rated yourself in the questionnaire as:

	PARTICIPATIVE	SUPPORTIVE	DEVELOPING	INNOVATIVE	OPEN
Very high	☑	☐	☐	☐	☐
High	☐	☐	☑	☑	☐
Average	☐	☑	☐	☐	☑
Slightly below average	☐	☐	☐	☐	☐
Well below average	☐	☐	☐	☐	☐

starts by giving individual course members behavioural feedback, and then brings them together to do some communal behavioural planning in their groups.

The feedback process begins, as it does in BOAC, by bringing all of the participating managers together in a general session where a trainer explains in detail what he has been up to whilst observing the group during the diagnostic period. He provides everybody with a copy of the particular behaviour analysis form he has been using, and carefully defines the way in which each category is used. He also shows the managers how the behaviour categories relate to the behavioural objectives for the training programme. (These are the objectives which were set by the top management of the part of the company from which the course members have come. They were arrived at as a direct result of the surveying activities, which preceded the design or mounting of any course.* Finally, the trainer runs through the actual format of the computer printouts and checks that everybody is clear about how to use the data.

The managers are then given their three printouts, which were described earlier, together with an individual project such as

---

Examine the behavioural feedback and then

● *set measurable aims for your own behaviour today*

● *produce some proposals for how you might increase the probability of achieving the aims*

They are given an hour to work on this alone, at the end of which they are required to have completed a BEHAVIOUR AIMS WORKSHEET, one copy for them and one copy for the trainer. One of these sheets is shown in FIGURE 19. They are encouraged to scatter around the building while undertaking this work, and the trainers make it clear that they are available throughout the period to give advice and counsel **if they are asked to do so by individual managers.** Trainers do not elbow-in on managers; they wait to be invited.

*See pages 84–8

19 behaviour aims worksheet

Please give a copy of this form to your coach at the start of the next task

NAME... DATE......................

Behavioural Category	Measurable Aims	Proposals for achieving aims
BUILDING	To increase to a level of 10% by next feedback	1 Listen carefully to other people's proposals 2 Write down the main points
		3 Check for compatibility with my own ideas 4 If possible, develop the existing proposal
DISAGREEING	To decrease to a level of 5%	1 Listen carefully 2 Check my understanding 3 If I am unable to agree, explain why and try to lead to an alternative proposal

Other measurable aims	Proposals for achieving aims
To bring my overall contribution rate up to 15%, + or − 3%, of the group's behaviour	I will ask to be group chairman for two successive sessions and then maintain the same sort of involvement as an ordinary group member

The emphasis is, therefore, on the individual. It is *his* behaviour that *he* is considering and it must be *his* proposals that lead to any attempted adjustment in that behaviour. The trainer finds himself in a counselling/consultancy role – giving guidance, reassurance, support, but always trying to bring the individual to a personal decision or proposal. We feel that to give the answer when asked *What should I do about this aspect of my behaviour?* is likely to be less than helpful in the long run – mainly because the individual has been robbed of the opportunity to arrive at his own conclusions, however similar they might have been to the coach's answer. An example of this is the individual who is concerned about his apparently high level of behaviours associated with questioning and seeking clarification. Through discussion, he arrives at a personal decision to cut severely this behaviour. As a result, he discovers through his activities in the subsequent projects, and in his next behavioural feedback, that his decision was not helping him, or the group, and he is then led to try an alternative strategy. The important thing is that he has learned by actually doing something and receiving knowledge of results or feedback – rather than being told the answer. In any event, there is no reason why the trainer should be expected to know the answer and, furthermore, if the trainer did generate all the proposals, then, in doing so, he would have robbed the manager of the valuable opportunity to learn from experience. After all, trainers aren't going to be hanging around armed with proposals back in the managerial work situation.

After an hour the managers reconvene in their groups (usually these are newly constituted groups incidentally. In chapter 6 Neil Rackham explains the advantages of mixing the course members at intervals throughout the course). The first project which faces them is usually one which encourages them to share information about their individual behavioural aims and proposals in such a way that they can actually support and help one another to achieve their aims. We find that most people require a supportive environment if they are to turn their proposals into action successfully. In ICL, we might structure the situation by giving the group the following project

Prepare a wall chart (they are encouraged to use large sheets of flip-chart paper) showing the actionable plan that will be followed by this group in order to assist individual group members to achieve the aims they have just set.

The measures of success for this project are

● *that the wall chart can be read by everyone in this group at a distance of 6 metres*

● *that the wall chart is displayed on a wall in this room by X o'clock (they are given 1-1¼ hours for this sort of project)*

● *that each individual recognises that the group plan caters adequately with at least one of his behavioural aims*

● *that by Y o'clock (this would be a time later in the day after three or four more projects have been tackled by the group) five individuals in this group can honestly claim that the group plan has been a help to them and give evidence to support this claim*

This group project, however worded (we have given only one version of it here, but for example with a group who are particularly skilled at setting clear, precise standards for their work, the trainer might leave out the measures entirely and leave it to them), is in reality another feedback task where individuals swop information about their own behavioural plans and gain information about their colleagues.

By involving the group in this way, we hope to avoid situations where unilateral action, however well intended, causes confusion. An example of this is the person who returned to his group after a feedback session and promptly turned his chair around, sitting with his back to the table. Investigation of this phenomena revealed that, far from withdrawing from the group, the person concerned was actioning his plan to avoid distracting himself and others through his habitual fidgeting with project materials that were on the table!

In ICL courses we, rather like BOAC, have some structured activities on the last day to do with planning behavioural and other changes in readiness for the return to the working situation. Since in ICL we run only tailor-made courses for managers who are drawn from the same part of the company on any given course, this sort of communal planning makes a great deal of sense. Because of this, the plans are often able to involve course members in various supportive activities in the work place itself.

SOME CONCLUSIONS

We started this chapter by saying how important a process feedback was and we have tried to show how in BOAC and ICL we tackle this in a responsible and sensible way. One measure of our success is obviously to do with the reactions of course members when they are exposed to this sort of behavioural data. In BOAC, where we have seen that the trainer runs feedback sessions with the group and with individuals, most course members find it initially a some-what daunting situation – understandably enough since it is probable that information about their style of interacting with other people will rarely, if ever, have been given to them in a systematic and objective way. However, almost without exception, members have responded to the situation in an extremely positive and favourable manner, and are usually reluctant to allow the trainer to close the feedback session. Data obtained from their session assessments confirms the high level of involvement and job relevance perceived in these sessions, although a few members are prepared to say that they did not enjoy it very much!

The comments of a senior BOAC manager, who recently visited a supervisors' course during its fourth day, perhaps summarise the typical course climate. Having spent three hours involved in activities partially designed by the course members themselves, he said that his most striking impression was the openness of members in their attitudes to discussion of personal behavioural characteristics and in their attempts to improve their interpersonal skills.

In ICL, where we have seen that the feedback tends to be entirely individually-oriented and structured in such a way that the trainer doesn't himself play such an active part in the feedback process, we have never known a manager who wasn't intrigued by the data. More importantly, we can't recall a single case where a manager has persisted in mis-interpreting the data in some way. Managers always spend the hour they have to pour over the printouts and set aims in the light of them very busily: it is very rare for them to go through a week without seeking advice from either the operations room staff or the trainers. ✳

chapter 6

INTERACTIVE SKILLS

mixing – a new technique in training

NEIL RACKHAM

In August 1967, Mr C was a middle manager with a large industrial concern in the north of England. To judge from his personnel record, he was well above average in ability although his performance was sometimes patchy. Still, he was only 34 and the firm's training manager was understandably anxious to offer him every help. Mr C's own diagnosis was simple enough: 'My problem,' he wrote, 'is not getting the best out of my people, but getting anything out of them at all. Unless I'm breathing down their necks, nothing gets done— so I am forced to do almost everything myself. Mr T's (the training manager's) priority should be to train my people to do an adequate job.'

THE TRAINING MANAGER, HOWEVER, SAW THINGS DIFFERENTLY In a memo to the personnel director, who was taking a direct interest in C's case, he wrote, 'The real difficulty is that although C sees this situation as arising from a failure in his subordinates, frankly, they mostly see the problem as C's failure to handle them sensibly . . . they say that C is not at all receptive to any ideas or initiatives other than his own and they feel that he is insensitive to their feelings and problems.'

Two weeks later, at a meeting between C and the training manager, C agreed that his own training need was for more effective interpersonal skills. After some discussion, it was agreed that T-group training would be most appropriate and, accordingly, C attended his first T-group in October 1967.

The results were dramatic. On his return most of his subordinates found him a changed man, describing him as *more considerate, more aware* and *better motivated* than before. Both the training manager and the personnel director were enormously impressed with the change, so they willingly accepted C's proposal to put 15 of his subordinates through similar training. Because it was impossible to release them all at once, it was decided to split the department into two groups; eight of them, together with C, attending an in-company T-group under the guidance of a most reputable and experienced T-group trainer in March 1968.

Again the results were dramatic and outsiders detected a significant improvement in the atmosphere, cheerfulness and efficiency of C and his department. Indeed, the seven departmental members who had not been on the T-group felt a little out of things and, as a result of their pressure, it was decided to bring the second in-company group forward from July to May 1968. Once again, C attended this T-group, which was run by the same trainer.

During this, his third T-group, something went seriously wrong. C broke down and, on the combined advice of the trainer and C's doctor, left before the end. He made a half-hearted attempt to return to work during the following weeks, but was unable to keep control of his job, or to interact with any of his subordinates. In August 1968 he started psychiatric treatment and, when last heard of in May 1970, was working in a different company in a much less senior position.

C's case was an exception, although a tragic one, and breakdowns of this order are an unlikely outcome from T-groups. However, his case raises an example of a most important problem for trainers and managers alike. Why did C emerge splendidly from two T-groups and not from the third? What was the difference between those group experiences? In a wider context, this problem is even more significant, as some examples will illustrate. Dr B was an outstandingly successful head of an R & D department. He moved to another company to do similar work and was a complete failure. Why? Mr W was sacked from a Bristol company for, in his own words, 'general incompetence and lack of ability'. Five years later he is a forward-looking director of one of the most successful companies in the United Kingdom.

How did such a transformation come about? Readers of this chapter will have similar experiences. They will know that when they are working with certain groups of people they get things done. However, we can all think of particular group situations – and committees are a favourite Aunt Sally – where, however hard we try, nothing is ever achieved. Why?

The group in which a person works exerts an enormous influence over that person and his behaviour patterns The answer to all these questions is that the group in which a person works exerts an enormous influence over that person and his behaviour patterns. Mr W said that working with the management group of his first company was 'like swimming in treacle'. 'In my present company', he said, 'we somehow clicked, and everything we did became exciting, worthwhile and, in commercial terms, enormously successful.' His case is a dramatic instance of how effectiveness is determined by the composition of a working group. The unfortunate case of C shows how the importance of group composition extends to the training situation. The first two T-groups C attended formed mini-environments with which he was compatible and his performance improved as a result. The third T-group provided an incompatible environment, so that C was not only unable to improve his

L

interpersonal skills, but also suffered serious personality damage.

Now C's case was, as I have said, extreme. But, as this chapter will show, the working or training environment in which a normal person is operating can exert an enormous effect on that person's behaviour patterns and his capacity to learn or to change. If we could control the learning environment, then we could profoundly influence people's capacity and motivation to learn. This chapter is written to show how

We can control major variables in the learning environment resulting in dramatic changes in people's behaviour patterns

we can control major variables in the learning environment which, until now, have not been controlled in any training situation, resulting in dramatic changes in people's behaviour patterns, involvement and learning.

This control over the composition of groups, and hence over what one could call the interactive environment, is an outcome of the research which started two years ago in BOAC and has since been continued in both BOAC and ICL. Other chapters in this book have described how our research explored some complex, but very fruitful, methods by which information about working groups could be collected, analysed and used to give people feedback on their performance. This same information can also be used to design new interactive environments (or if you don't like jargon – to choose new mixtures of people). We call this process MIXING, and the rest of this chapter explains why we developed mixing in the first place and how it works.

In our early attempts to produce a powerful but controlled type of interactive skills training, we were faced with a problem which is common to every form of training involving people working together in groups. The size of this problem can be seen from the following extract from my own research notes, written in November 1968 when we had recognised the problem but before we had produced any of the answers.

The crux of the matter is that the most powerful way to train people to work together or interact effectively is to train them in groups, whether T-groups or the whole variety of structured groups such as Coverdale or the sort of thing Peter Honey is doing in BOAC. But group-centred training is both risky and uneconomical. Risky *because we can't control it – T-groups especially although other forms aren't much better, just that the consequences from lack of control are less dramatic; their biggest risk is that they may have no effect whatsoever. Even worse, group-centred training is, as a consequence of being uncontrolled, also unpredictable. So you may have a group which works splendidly, or, more often, doesn't change at all. We can't predict which groups will change any more than we can predict in advance which T-groups will blow up.* Uneconomical *because, in any group session, and at any moment, what is going on in the group will not be equally relevant or useful to all group members. So, for long periods, group-centred training may be an uneconomical use of time for the majority of individuals. Again, neither we nor they can control this, except in the crudest terms. The aim of any research here must be to keep the power of group-centred training while reducing its risky and uneconomical aspects. Ultimate objectives – power with safety, reliability and economy.*

The use of behaviour analysis and feedback, which is discussed in earlier chapters, gave us only a very limited control over the progress of each group, but it did demonstrate to us one very important, and very disturbing, fact. In the early courses we studied, some groups showed significant and positive changes both in their perceptions and in their behaviour patterns, while other groups showed no improvement at all. Now, statistically speaking, of 16 people on a course which is divided into two groups, it is most unlikely that eight randomly-chosen individuals put into one group would all improve their performance significantly, while none of the remaining eight people assigned equally randomly to the other group would show any significant improvement at all. Yet this happened on more than one occasion. The only reasonable explanation was that learning, or behaviour change, depended on the composition of the group. If an individual was in the right group he would improve his performance – if he was in the wrong group he wouldn't.

I write about this simple discovery as though it was a great revelation. It shouldn't have been: the examples earlier in this chapter testify to the variety of situations in which performance is group-dependent. Social psychologists have pointed this out for many years, yet nobody in the training world had done anything about it. Even today, none of the group-centred training systems currently available does anything significant to control the most important aspect of their training situation – the composition of each group being trained. Because group-centred training is still at the stage of alchemy rather than science, it has so far been easy to disregard inconvenient discoveries of this nature.

It is, of course, easy to criticise the failure of various forms of interactive skills training to face up to the central problem of group composition. Yet this failure is hardly surprising in view of the difficulties involved. In order to change the composition of groups, it would be essential to collect a great deal of data about every individual and their patterns of interaction. Such data is difficult to collect and, once collected, only considerable and costly experiment can show the best way to use it.

However, in BOAC, and subsequently also in ICL, we were ideally placed to experiment with group composition. Behaviour analysis, coupled with measures of each individual's perceptions, generated up to 50 000 data items in a five-day course and provided us with a rich supply of data to use in the difficult business of learning how to mix groups. Our objectives in both companies during this experimental phase could be summed up in the terms of the research notes as 'power with safety, reliability and economy'.

As earlier chapters have described, the first phase of training is diagnostic, with individuals working in groups at a whole variety of interactive activities including case studies, discussions, structured or unstructured tasks and role-playing; all chosen to be intrinsically relevant to their training needs. During this phase, their behaviour is monitored using various forms of behaviour analysis. An example of how group mixing is used during this diagnostic period will demonstrate how behaviour change is affected by the differences in the work environment produced by changes in group composition.

CONTRIBUTION-RATE MIXES

The BOAC course which started on 6 July 1970, contained
a typical diagnostic stage mix and provides the data for
this example. There were 21 course members, randomly
divided into three groups of seven. During the first day of
the course, it became evident that of the 21 course members,
there were a number of particularly dominant individuals
who were making, on average, twice as many contributions
as other members of their respective groups. Similarly,
there were some very low contributors who were each
making less than one third of the average contribution rate.
This very significant difference was growing even greater
as the day wore on. From our experience on earlier courses,
we knew that there was a high probability that this diver-
gence would continue, so that the initial disparity between
the highest and the lowest contribution rate would grow
greater later in the course. We also knew that these disproportionately diverse levels of contribution were likely to
lead to

● drop-outs from the low contributors who had lost
interest in the course
● protracted leadership battles among high contributors
which were unlikely to be resolved within the five course
days
● a generally low overall level of perceived satisfaction
and learning by group members
● a below average overall amount of behaviour change
resulting from the course

We therefore decided to counter this trend by group mixing.
We selected the seven highest contributors and put them
in a group together. Similarly the seven lowest contributors
were taken from the groups in which they were working
and put together in another group. This left seven people
from the three original groups who were all average contributors and they were put together to make up the third
group. FIGURE 20 shows how this mix was constituted.
Our experience was that our action would create a high
pressure environment for the high contributors where they
would quickly discover the disadvantages of their dominating
behaviour. The low contributors were in the reverse

20] how a contribution rate mix works

IN ANY GROUP OF PEOPLE BEING TRAINED THERE ARE...

high contributors
who say a great deal, tend
to dominate the group's
activities and show little
behaviour change.

mid contributors
who say an average amount
and tend to learn new
behaviour patterns more
quickly than do high or low
contributors.

low contributors
who say very little, tend to
lose involvement easily
and show very little
behaviour change.

IN THE BOAC EXAMPLE, THE ORIGINAL GROUPS WERE...

WE MIXED THESE RANDOM GROUPS TO FORM

high contributors
said half as much,
started to show positive
behaviour changes.

mid contributors
carried on much as before,
continuing to show positive
behaviour changes.

low contributors
said twice as much,
became more involved,
started to show positive
behaviour changes.

The group in which a person works exerts an enormous influence over that person and his behaviour patterns situation: because their group contained no dominant people, we believed that they would find it easier to contribute and their contribution rate would rise dramatically. We did not anticipate any significant change for the middle contribution level group. The actual changes are shown in FIGURE 21. The high contributors' group started, as one might anticipate, with a spectacular session in which everyone was talking at once and attempting to dominate the group. However, they soon realised that, although they could get away with this behaviour in their original groups, it was not going to work among other high contributors. As FIGURE 21 shows, the result was a very significant fall in their contribution rate. This fall was important because high contributors tend to be very resistant to behaviour change. One reason for this is that they try to make the rest of the group change to conform with them, rather than change themselves to adapt to the group. The effect of the high contribution group was, as we predicted, to reduce individuals' contribution rate and to begin changing their behaviour patterns which, in the original groups, had been very resistant to change.

21 changes in contribution rate caused by mixing groups

	average contribution levels		
	4 sessions before mix in original groups	4 sessions during mix in contribution rate groups	4 sessions after mix in original groups
high contribution group	1 289	658	1 070
mid contribution group	772	624	851
low contribution group	302	603	366

The mid contributors, when put together, tended to behave much as they had done before, showing a slight drop in their contribution rate. Behaviour change, in the early

Interactive skills training, as described by contributors to this book, becomes one of the cheapest, as well as the most powerful, forms of training when the numbers being trained are relatively large

stages of a course, tends to be greatest among mid contributors and in this course it continued at about the same rate in the mixed as in the original groups.

The low contribution group started the first session very quietly, each group member waiting for the others to make the running. As soon as it became plain that there were no particularly vocal members in the group, members' contribution rates increased dramatically (FIGURE 21). Low contributors, left in their original random groups, tend to say less as time goes on. Until the group is skilful enough to involve its low contributors, their enjoyment and involvement falls off and they show very little behaviour change. We therefore wished to ensure that low contributors were in an environment where perceived enjoyment and involvement would be as high as possible. The perceptual measures which we used to rate each session showed that we had succeeded in this respect: in the mixed group, low contributors ratings for enjoyment and involvement showed a significant improvement. Moreover, significant changes in behaviour patterns started to take place.

The dramatic changes in the mixed groups are an interesting indication of the power of mixing to influence group behaviour. However, the most important test of the contribution mix is the effect which it has on individuals when they return to their original groups. In this example

● high contributors decreased from original levels by 17 per cent
● mid contributors increased from original levels by 9 per cent
● low contributors increased from original levels by 21 per cent

The before and after behaviour change in the high and low groups is statistically very significant and is the more remarkable because, without mixing, there was a high probability of the opposite change – with high contributors increasing their rates and low contributors decreasing.

The contribution rate mix is an example of an area where many trainers could use mixing to immediate advantage. In recent months, as details of this technique have become available, various companies, technical colleges and business schools have started to plan course designs based on contribution rates mixes. In particular, it seems that this kind of mix is most useful where a course contains a significant proportion of syndicate or discussion work. On the basis of contribution rates, syndicate groups can be constructed which, if nothing else, will ensure an even opportunity for all members to participate.

Because of its ease of use and immediate potential for application, it is worth examining the contribution rate mix in more detail. The case study, this time, is from a two group ICL management course run during October 1970.

22 changes in contribution rate in an ICL two group course

| | contribution levels | | |
	pre-mix original groups	during mix contribution groups	post-mix original groups
high contributors	736	697	672
low contributors	372	552	499

FIGURE 22 shows a contrast with the BOAC study which is outlined in FIGURE 21. The ICL example has been chosen to show how the change in overall contribution rate from a two group course is less during a contribution rate mix than from a three group course. The reason for this is straightforward: the more groups on a course, the more options for placing any individual into the optimum interactive environment. So a mid contributor in a two group course must fall either into the high or the low contribution group, which reduces the power of the mix. At the other extreme, we are contemplating a contribution rate mix for a seven group business school course, where the existence of seven groups will allow us to construct groups where a very fine and very powerful discrimination can be made between different designs of group environments.

Mixing is very attractive in terms of its cost effectiveness. Unlike most forms of training, mixing-based training becomes increasingly powerful with greater numbers

This is one of the unique features of mixing, which makes the technique very attractive in terms of its cost effectiveness. The greater the number of groups being trained simultaneously, the greater the number of mixing options and the more powerful each mix. So, unlike most forms of training, which reduce in effectiveness as the number of participants grows, mixing-based training becomes increasingly powerful with greater numbers. Moreover, the relatively costly unit overhead of data processing and fluid design decisions from a central control room, is greatly reduced. As a result, interactive skills training as described by contributors to this book, becomes one of the cheapest, as well as the most powerful, forms of training when the numbers being trained are relatively large.

Returning to the ICL case study, the changes in contribution rate can be broken down into component behaviours. By doing this we can see whether, in changing the overall rate of behaviour, there was also any shift in the underlying pattern. FIGURE 23 shows the mix when broken down into the component behaviours of the ICL general behaviour analysis. The numbers in each cell of the table are the actual numbers of each behaviour recorded during an equivalent sampling period before, during and after the mix. So, taking the first behaviour category, SEEKING SUGGESTIONS, as an example, the low contributors' group had made:

● 26 seeking suggestion contributions in original groups before the mix

● 35 seeking suggestion contributions in the low contributors' group

● 45 seeking suggestion contributions in original groups after the mix

The high contributors' group had made:

● 49 seeking suggestion contributions in original groups before the mix

● 49 seeking suggestion contributions in the high contributors' group

● 41 seeking suggestion contributions in original groups after the mix

23 behaviour category breakdown of ICL contribution rate mix

	SEEKING SUGGESTIONS		CAUGHT PROPOSALS		ESCAPED PROPOSALS		BUILDING	
LOW CONTRIBUTORS	26 BEFORE MIX	35 DURING MIX / (45) AFTER MIX	70	95 / 68	5	5 / 4	13	13 / 14
HIGH CONTRIBUTORS	49	49 / 41	131	110 / 122	6	6 / 8	39	(18) / 37
Significant differences between groups	sig before mix	not sig after mix	sig before mix	sig after mix	not sig before mix	not sig after mix	sig before mix	sig after mix

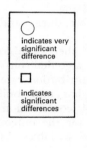

○ indicates very significant difference

☐ indicates significant differences

	DISAGREEING		SEEKING CONFIRMATION		SUPPORTING		SEEKING CLARIFICATION	
	5	(33) / (12)	14	(56) / 40	39	41 / [52]	81	84 / (116)
	25	18 / 21	55	60 / (31)	65	(143) / [49]	124	104 / 130
	sig before mix	sig after mix	sig before mix	not sig after mix	sig before mix	not sig after mix	sig before mix	not sig after mix

UNSTRUCTURED CONTRIBUTIONS		OTHER BEHAVIOUR		UNINVITED OFFERINGS		MULTI-SPEAK		TOTAL BEHAVIOUR	
1	(14) / 6	87	104 / [106]	17	(35) / [25]	14	(37) / 11	372	(552) / (499)
3	1 / 3	163	139 / 181	36	29 / 31	40	(20) / (18)	736	697 / [672]
not sig before mix	not sig after mix	sig before mix	not sig after mix	sig before mix	not sig after mix	sig before mix	not sig after mix	sig before mix	sig after mix

So, before the mix there was a significant difference between high and low contributors on this behaviour, with high contributors making about twice as many contributions in this category. After the mix, there was no significant difference between high and low contributors, the effect of the mix having been to increase the low contributors' frequency of response for this behaviour. A close study of FIGURE 23 will show a number of shifts in the behaviour patterns of both the high and the low group.

The results in FIGURE 23 are not, of course, absolutely typical of the outcome of any contribution rate mix. We have found that several variables influence the specific behaviour patterns in the mix, including

● the duration of the mix
● the point in the course at which it takes place
● the type of participant, eg managerial, supervisory
● the number of groups available for mixing
● the sort of activities groups work at before, during and after the mix

Because of the influence of these and other variables, we cannot, either in BOAC or in ICL, state a golden rule which specifies the exact outcome of every contribution rate mix. However, because each organisation has now built up considerable data-based experience of contribution rate mixes, we can state probability levels for the outcome of any mix, given a knowledge of the above variables. As each organisation's experience grows, so it becomes increasingly possible to specify and control key variables influencing the outcome of group mixes.

Not all mixes are based on contribution rates. Indeed, most of the experience in both BOAC and ICL has been concerned with much more complex and specific mixing systems. However, because anybody can mix groups on a contribution basis, merely by counting the number of contributions each person makes, we feel it worthwhile to put special emphasis on this type of mix. At least one trainer has carried out his own contribution rate mix by noting frequency of contribution on the back of an envelope. He mixed groups with the intention of making syndicate work more useful and, although he lacks the comprehensive data recording systems of either BOAC or ICL, he subjectively reports his experiments as '*an amazing success*'.

What are these other types of mixing? The general class which we use most are negative mixes – that is, groups mixed on the basis of a behaviour which we are trying to reduce in frequency. So, for example, if we wished to reduce disagreeing we would constitute a group of those high on disagreeing behaviour. By putting the high disagreers together for a time, their frequency of disagreeing behaviour falls – and continues to fall when they return to their original groups. We have used mixes of this sort in both companies to reduce such behaviours as defending/attacking, difficulty stating, criticising and interrupting.

But beware! All of the behaviours mentioned in the previous paragraph tend to fall off as the course progresses, whether negative mixes are used or not. So in BOAC, we decided to test whether negative mixes were really doing any good, or whether we had been fooled into thinking that the fall in negative behaviours was due to mixing, when this fall would have happened anyway.

We took the results from negative behaviour mixes on six courses and compared them with unmixed control groups who were also high on these behaviours. FIGURE 24 shows the result. The unmixed groups did indeed reduce their level of negative behaviour by 8 per cent. However, the groups who went through a negative behaviour mix, reduced their level by 26 per cent over a similar period.

Again, as with contribution rate mixes, both BOAC and ICL are building up data which will allow them to predict the outcome of negative behaviour mixes with increasing accuracy.

At this point, anybody without first hand experience of our courses might easily view us as rather unscrupulous manipulators, playing an elaborate game of behavioural chess, with unwitting course members as our pawns. This was once brought home to me with a jolt, when a visitor to the ops room revealed, 'It's not what I'd expected. Somehow I'd always imagined a secret underground laboratory, with men in white coats and sinister foreign accents'. He was mildly disappointed to discover that all ops room functions,

Unscrupulous manipulators, playing an elaborate game of behavioural chess

24 general effect of negative behaviour mixes

	average level of negative behaviours used as basis for mix		
	four hours behaviour sampling before mix	four hours behaviour sampling during mix	four hours behaviour sampling after mix
composite of 6 negative behaviour mixes from different BOAC courses	589	535	436
% change from pre-mix		—9	—26
average level of negative behaviours in similar sampling periods for unmixed control group	524	502	486
% change from pre-mix		—5	—8

including group mixing, were completely open so that course members could, and did, walk in at any time to ask about what we were doing and why. In ICL, course members are sometimes given the behavioural data and asked to decide on the mix for themselves – and in both companies there is a complete openness between trainers and course members in terms of mixing and its effects.

The use of contribution rate and negative behaviour mixes has given considerable power to the form of training which these chapters describe. As a result, we can now achieve four times the overall amount of behaviour change in a given course than we were achieving two years ago when these developments started. What is more, our knowledge of the control mechanisms – and especially mixing – allows us to focus this change as we require it.

This chapter opened with the case of C, whose third T-group proved so traumatic. Our knowledge of mixing would now enable us to avoid such a situation and testimony to our developing skill in this respect is that over 300 BOAC supervisors have gone through this powerful form of training without a single case of significant emotional disturbance. ICL can also claim similarly impressive figures. But control is a double-edged weapon. Just as we can control the training to prevent the irreversible conflict of incompatible behaviour patterns, so, if we chose, we could build up such conflict. Such a mix would be designed to expose an individual to group situations with which behaviour analysis had shown him to be incompatible. So our capacity to save C would also give us the power to make his situation worse.

I hope that this sounds sinister, because it is meant to draw attention to a very nasty reality which we must all face. In combination, the control mechanisms described in this and earlier chapters, provide a powerful system for producing behaviour change. But unlike change in more restricted areas of job behaviour, such as Algol programming, or the ability to understand discounted cash flow systems, changes in people's interactive behaviour extend beyond their work environment into all areas of their lives.

Changes in people's interactive behaviour extend beyond their environment into all areas of their lives

We must ask ourselves what moral justification we have for putting people through an experience powerful enough to change not only their work behaviour, but also wider and more personal aspects of their social interactions. Because existing forms of interactive skills training are relatively weak, this has not previously been a burning question. But the work which has been carried out in BOAC and ICL points the way to a future where extremely powerful forms of training will exist – and such power has capacity for misuse. For this reason, a code of practice is rapidly becoming necessary and it would seem appropriate to end this chapter – which introduced a new training technique – with a proposed code to control and guide its use.

New and powerful forms of interactive skills training will be acceptable only when **all of the following conditions are met**

● The training method must be capable of considerable control, either by the integration of behaviour analysis, feedback and mixing, or by some similarly exact mechanism.

● It must be based on systematic, quantified and explicit data, not on anecdotal observation.

● The portion of this data describing any individual must be freely available to that individual.

● The training must be under the direct and immediate control of highly qualified and experienced trainers who subscribe to a code such as this one.

● Each individual should go through a gentler part 1 stage to assess his suitability for a more intense experience.

● All those accepted for a more powerful experience should be warned privately and individually in advance of the training of the likely risks, consequences and problems. They should be given every opportunity to withdraw discreetly or be offered the choice of alternative training.

● Once on the course, provision must be made for individuals to opt out, without question or loss of face, either into a lower pressure situation designed for the purpose, or by leaving the training entirely.

● Stringent measures should be taken to ensure that all matters arising on and from the course are treated as strictly confidential, both by trainers and by group members. ✳

the trainer's guide to successful plagiarism

PETER HONEY

If you have lasted the course I expect you could be
feeling pretty overwhelmed by now. You will have
read about behaviour analysis categories,
computer-assisted feedback, operations rooms
manned by behavioural scientists, and lots more.
In this chapter I am going to show you how to apply
something of these new methods with minimal
resources. When I talk of resources, I'm thinking of
money, people and time. In so doing, I shall make
my colleagues wince because, inevitably, the starter
suggestions I shall make fall a long way short of
the sort of standards we have become used to in
ICL and BOAC. My colleagues will wince because
the standards they are used to are not absurdly high.
I am prepared to leave them wincing if I can do
something to give you a leg up into the interactive
skills area. At the very start we said that our
purpose in publishing at all has been to encourage
trainers to implement, and put into everyday use,
some of the new methods which we have developed
in our work. Neil Rackham actually invited you to
'plagiarise, copy, adapt, modify or develop anything
which you read'. And this is surely sensible. You
will have noticed our own unashamed references to
plagiarism throughout the previous chapters. The
existence of this current chapter should reinforce
our sincerity in making such an invitation and,
make it more likely that you will accept.

We must take steps to ensure before a course that any behavioural changes brought about during it are suitable ones in terms of the on-the-job working situation

THIS CHAPTER IS NOT IN ANY SENSE A REPLACEMENT FOR THE previous six. Consequently, this will mean that I shall not pause to re-explain things, but I am going to write it in sections so that you will know which previous chapter to refer back to. In writing this chapter at all I have two sorts of trainers in mind, or, more accurately, two sorts of training situations in mind. Firstly, all those trainers who use syndicates, or any form of group activity, as a means of achieving learning objectives, but not necessarily to achieve objectives in the interactive skills area. Trainers who use case study methods where syndicates are required to discuss matters and come up with recommendations, and trainers who use, for example, business games can, we believe, increase their effectiveness considerably by incorporating, in a simplified way if need be, one or two of the methods.

Secondly, I have in mind all the trainers who haven't a hope of acquiring the sorts of resources that have been referred to in the ICL and BOAC descriptions and yet who want to start working in the interactive skills area. For example, you will have noticed that in both BOAC and ICL one full-time trainer for each group of seven or eight is a must. How many of you can stomach that when you think of your own slender resources? But take heart! I regularly run a five-day interactive skills course for the Atomic Energy Research Establishment at Harwell entirely single-handed with two, sometimes three, groups and still manage to provide a satisfactory, though depleted, behaviour analysis feedback service. It can be done and I'm out to show you how.

If by any chance you are a large company trainer with all the appliances and means to boot ready to swing into action on interactive skills activities, then the earlier chapters will clearly be more of an inspiration to you than this one.

One final introductory point before embarking on the do-it-yourself stuff. I am going to try to avoid peppering this chapter with *it all depends* type qualifications. Instead I shall assume that you already know, and will not suddenly forget, that what you do and don't do all depends on, for example, your particular situation, your particular training objectives, and so on. You will find, therefore, that I concentrate on throwing up a number of alternatives and leave it to you to sort out which, if any, are the most appropriate to your particular circumstances. So I will try to cut down the frequency of *it all depends*, so long as you promise to remember that **it does all depend.**

Let's take things in the order we are used to. We will start by looking at what you can plagiarise from the pre-course activities like surveying and then move on to behaviour analysing, feeding-back and, finally, mixing.

PRE-COURSE ACTIVITIES

I am very keen on pre- and for that matter, post-course activities. So keen that I sometimes convince myself that the run-up to a course is more important, in terms of the influence it has on managerial behaviour, than the course itself. The suggestions I have to make in this section of the chapter are primarily directed at the trainer who wants to start working in the interactive skills area, but they could give others some ideas also.

Two important starter thoughts have been a big help to me.

The more potent your training, the more it matters that the changes are appropriate

The first one is that the more potent your training, in other words the better it is at bringing about behavioural change, then the more it matters that the changes are appropriate and in the required direction. This means that somehow or other we must take steps to ensure before a course that any behavioural changes brought about during it are suitable ones in terms of the on-the-job working situation. This realisation alone would seem enough to warrant a flurry of pre-course activities, but couple it with the second point I have to make and it should all prove irresistible!

The second thought is that people will not learn to change their behaviour unless they want to. Since we are all relatively rotten at knowing how to get people to want to do whatever it is that we want them to do, it is not unusual to devote 50 per cent or more of the time on a course trying to get participants to the point where they want to learn. How much better to shunt the efforts to motivate the learners right out of the course and into the pre-course situation. Accordingly, all the suggestions I have to make now are

**People will not learn
to change their
behaviour unless
they want to**

aimed at pulling off both these purposes; finding out what is appropriate whilst motivating people at the same time. I haven't got anything startling to reveal. In fact, what I can suggest is a right old slog. Start by getting people hooked on interactive behaviour. Keep talking about it when you have conversations with managers. Ask them to describe the ways in which they observe effective, as opposed to less effective, managers behaving in interactive situations. When they say *with confidence* or *decisively*, quiz them on the precise ways in which effective managers behave, in different situational settings, to earn labels such as confident and decisive. It's better still if you can ask these sorts of questions during a series of structured interviews with managers or groups of managers. I have found that just about everybody gets involved in this sort of thinking quite quickly. They are enormously complimented that you are consulting them about such things and that such close attention is being paid to their personal philosophies and ideas.

Make sure that you take detailed notes. Write down as much as you can get verbatim. Continually plug the point that you want to get nitty-gritty behavioural data and not glib stuff about managerial qualities and styles. It is a big help to feed them with situations in your bid to track down relatively specific behaviours. Ask 'How does this manager you have in mind behave when he runs meetings with his subordinates?'. 'How does he behave when appraising people's performance?'. 'How does he behave when informing his boss that something has gone wrong?', and so on.

After you have assembled data from as many people as you can, either compile it into a questionnaire or produce lists of behaviours under situational headings. There are sure to be discrepancies in the lists, so keep showing them to people and asking them which behaviours they think are most closely associated with effectiveness. When they elect their preferences, ask them why they feel that such and such a behaviour is more likely to be effective. Take notes again. In fact, I recommend you to keep an exercise book marked INTERACTIVE BEHAVIOUR and carry it everywhere with you, ready to enter the latest gem.

The alternative is to compile all the ideas you have collected into a behavioural checklist or questionnaire.

Make it a ticks in boxes things like this

Delegates tasks in such a way that his people know precisely what is expected of them. ☐☐☐☐☐ Delegates tasks in such a way that his people are confused about what is expected of them.

---

or like this

How often should a manager speak to his people in a manner which discourages questions from them?

☐ always
☐ often
☐ occasionally
☐ seldom
☐ never

---

or like this

When a manager is asked by his boss how things are going, he should

a say that everything is fine and leave it at that

b give him a progress report and emphasise the things which are proving troublesome or difficult

c give him a progress report and emphasise the things which are going well and proving successful

---

– or like any of the numerous sound questionnaire constructions.

Since questionnaires are unpopular, don't send it out to the people you want to fill it in. Much better to make an appointment and take it with you. This has the advantage of bringing you and them together yet again. If you are on the spot, you can also introduce the questionnaire, cope with their queries or irritations, get them to complete it there and then, make sure that they don't dwell unduly

over some points and dash over others, make sure that they
don't go back through it changing their mind, and so on.

Whatever you do, make sure that you anchor the thoughts
of the man who is completing the questionnaire firmly to
reality. That is to say, get him to think about his boss's
behaviour, or one of his subordinate manager's behaviour,
or the behaviour of a manager he works closely with and
considers effective. There is no need for people to identify
whom they have in mind (this isn't a witch-hunt), but it is
vital that they latch firmly on to actual behaviour rather
than floating off into idealistic, Utopian thoughts.

I usually conduct surveys of this kind by topping and tailing
the organisation. Briefly, what happens is that every manager
is visited separately on two occasions split in time by two
days or more. On the first occasion he might complete a
questionnaire with the behaviour of, say, his most effective
subordinate manager in mind, and, on the second, with his
least effective subordinate manager's behaviour as the
bench mark. When all the participants have completed
two questionnaires in this way, it is relatively easy to do some
statistical analysis on each item, in order to determine
whether it is a significant distinguisher between effective and
less effective managers in the organisation. This whittles
down the number of items considerably. Some fail to show
significance because they were poor items in the first place,
and some because the behaviour they describe was shared by
both effective and less effective managers.

Once you have got some results from all these participative
investigatory activities, share them widely with everyone
who has been involved. Take any opportunity you reasonably
can to interest people in the findings. Discuss their implications for the organisation and particularly ask people to
consider whether the behavioural picture which emerges is,
in their judgment, appropriate to the organisation's objectives and forward plans. Ask them if the behaviours which
come out as significant distinguishers are indeed the make-
or-break behaviours needed by effective managers in the
future.

It is in this sort of climate that I have found that managers
are willing, and a great deal more able, to hammer out what

work-related behavioural objectives they want any subsequent training courses to achieve. For me this is a very important point. It seems to me absolutely fundamental that managers play their proper part in stating what they want to get out of a course in precise, measurable terms and planning how they, the managers, are going to apply the measures. This is really healthy involvement and anything you can think of doing to bring it about will be worth the effort.

It sounds a lot of work. It is a lot of work. It need not absorb your full time attention. In fact, you might do well to start on this behavioural quest by running it in parallel with other duties which take you out and about in the work place. If you simply haven't the time or the nerve to tackle the pre-course activities I have described so far, then there are a number of alternatives open to you.

Try trotting round to people with a list of candidates for a behaviour analysis form (some suggestions are given later) and get them to say which categories are relevant, in their opinion, to the organisation and, of those, which ones should be increased in managers and which decreased. This is awfully subjective and without the advantages on a firmer data base such as a survey provides, but at least it involves people in the selection of the behaviour analysis categories you will subsequently use.

Another alternative is to start sitting in at management meetings and doing some behaviour analysis. Or, see if you can arrange to trail a manager around every now and again and behaviour analyse him as he copes with the interactive situations which come his way. I have got lots more to say about behaviour analysing in the next section so I won't dwell on it now except to say that it lends itself superbly well to the work situation. As an information collecting device it is just as suitable during real interactive situations as it is during contrived training ones. In fact, it is an excellent way of collecting hard factual, detailed information about how people actually do behave in the countless interface situations in which their job involves them. It cuts straight through all the difficulties of being dependent upon what people say about how they behave.

A final alternative pre-course activity aimed at giving you

behavioural data and involving people before you reach the stage of running a course, is to get at interface situations and interactive behaviour via people's objectives or key tasks. This is only really feasible if there is some sort of MbO scheme in existence. The way I do it is to sit down with a manager and, using his objectives as the starting point, quiz him about the interactive situations he will be in as he tackles the various tasks involved in achieving an objective. Every objective reveals several different key interface situations and these, in turn, can then be broken down into key interactive behaviours. Do this in conversation with the manager by asking such things as 'In what way will you have to behave in that situation if you are to achieve this objective?'. When you have done this with a few people, you have the beginnings of a list of interactive behaviours which are closely associated with the achievement of agreed objectives. This list can then serve as the basis for your deliberations over what the training objectives should be and over what behaviour analysis categories to use.

BEHAVIOUR ANALYSING

You will have gathered from chapter 4 on COLLECTING BEHAVIOURAL DATA that the method we call behaviour analysing is, fundamentally, a crude running-tally mark system, which succeeds in breaking interactive behaviour down into small bits or categories. (Small that is, in relation to things like managerial qualities and managerial styles. Terry Morgan distinguished very usefully between gross behavioural styles and specific skills in the first chapter.) In fact, I think behaviour analysis is *so* crude and *so* simple that it is surprising that more people are not actively engaged in doing it. I suspect that the reason why it isn't more prevalent is because the actual act of behaviour analysing is very hard work and, after a period of initial entrancement, is a crashing bore.

A word of warning however. Notice how carefully BOAC and ICL train their coaches, particularly in the business of behaviour analysing. If you are on your own you will have to train yourself. Practise whenever you can – sitting in at meetings, watching a play on television, listening to tape recordings, and so on. If you have a colleague, then try behaviour analysing the same event separately and then do a careful comparison of similarities and discrepancies. Tape, or video tape, recordings are particularly useful, since you can play it, or parts of it in dispute, back as often as you need in order to resolve your differences.

The first tip is not to start off with 12 or 13 behaviour categories. Try two or four. And start with some fairly straightforward ones like AGREEING, DISAGREEING, ASKING FOR CLARIFICATION, GIVING CLARIFICATION. At least, if you are a beginner, and you find out that the ratio of DISAGREEING to AGREEING in a group or in an individual is 5:1, then you have collected an important bit of information which would have been only a vague impression without the discipline of a blow-by-blow tally-mark recording system.

I think the important thing about choosing your behaviour analysis categories is to relax and feel free to experiment. Once you get the bug you will think of trying all sorts of things. You can even collect data about the incidence of laughter in a group, about eye-contact, about how many times people say *I* and how many times they say *we*, and so on. You can develop your own theories about what behaviours are facilitatory in a group and what are inhibitory and then collect behavioural information to support or refute your ideas. The fundamental point to hang on to is that behaviour is observable, and what is observable is amenable to this sort of analytical treatment by an alert observer.

If you are going to start by experimenting with a few behaviour categories of your own selection, rather than getting your target population to do the choosing, then here is a list of some of the categories that I have used. You can use it as a starter. Incidentally, I have found that coping with 14 categories at once is my absolute limit, and that 10 or 11 is far more comfortable. This is an important point, since it is self-defeating to have a magnificent list of behaviours which you can't use anything like accurately enough. Much better to use say six really competently.

Here is the list:

SEEKING IDEAS/SUGGESTIONS AND PROPOSALS – procedural

SEEKING IDEAS/SUGGESTIONS AND PROPOSALS – task
BRINGING IN
SEEKING INFORMATION
GIVING IDEAS, SUGGESTIONS AND PROPOSALS
PROVIDING INFORMATION
CAUGHT PROPOSALS
ESCAPED PROPOSALS
INNOVATING
ASKED INFORMATION GIVING
UNASKED INFORMATION GIVING
SEEKING CLARIFICATION
SEEKING TO ESTABLISH LEVELS OF UNDERSTANDING
TESTING UNDERSTANDING
GIVING CLARIFICATION
SUMMARISING
HOLDING
SOLIDIFYING
REGURGITATING
MAKING EXPLANATIONS
SEEKING CONFIRMATION AND SUPPORT
SEEKING TO ESTABLISH LEVELS OF AGREEMENT
SUPPORTING
AGREEING
BUILDING
SYNTHESISING
ASKING QUESTIONS – sub-divided as you like, eg leading,
open-ended etc
DISAGREEING
CRITICISING
STATING DIFFICULTIES
IDENTIFYING PROBLEMS
DEFENDING
ATTACKING
ADMITTING INADEQUACY
BACK TRACKING
JUMPING THE GUN
UNSTRUCTURED CONTRIBUTIONS
INTERRUPTING
TALKING-OVER
RAMBLING

MULTI-SPEAKING

SHUTTING-OUT

OVERT REFERENCES – to whatever you want, eg setting objectives, setting standards, planning

Another very obvious bit of BAing you can do is to focus on the relative frequency and duration of people's verbal contributions. Simply list the people's names on a piece of paper and put a check mark next to a name each time that person says something. You can measure duration by putting down a check mark at fixed intervals – say every three or five seconds – as long as the speaker continues. After a time you can summarise the data you have assembled to show who has talked, how often, and how much of the total available time he has used. You will also have access to who used short communications and who spoke for long periods.

When observing dyad interactions, the actual example was concerned with the development of appraisal interviewing skills, I have just about managed to do both. That is, I have categorised the verbal exchanges between the two people and also managed to do a frequency analysis. But I have to admit that this was only possible by using a 10-second interval between check marks. It has been worth it though, for being entirely dependent upon the total number of behaviours recorded can be misleading. For example, I have found that short appraisal interviews will produce a total of 52 recorded behaviours for the appraiser and only 34 for the appraisee. This could lead people to erroneously conclude that the appraiser did far more talking than the appraisee. But put alongside those figures the additional data from the 10-second check and we have 35 check marks for the appraiser and 78 for the appraisee. The interpretation is now clear; the appraiser made more contributions but they were short and snappy; the appraisee did most of the talking.

There is no doubt that ideally you should assemble behavioural data about a group over quite a long period before you consider using the information with any certainty as to its reliability. Notice that both BOAC and ICL have diagnostic periods on their five-day courses which are a day to two days long. Furthermore, it is of course preferable to have a trainer sitting in with a group doing the behaviour analysis on a full-time, uninterrupted basis. However, you might be forced to break both these rules because of serious resource deprivation. If so, then proceed very cautiously, treat the data you collect as tentative, and stress its short-comings to your course members quite openly. If you have a couple of syndicates at work on some project or another and you want to provide a limited behaviour analysis service, then try doing it by oscillating between the groups. It is vital to behaviour analyse for a fixed time period in both groups if you want the data to be comparable. What I usually do is produce a schedule for myself like this

syndicate 1	syndicate 2
BA for 4 mins	
	BA for 4 mins
BA for 8 mins	
	BA for 8 mins
BA for 10 mins	
	BA for 10 mins
BA for 10 mins	
	BA for 10 mins

and so on until the end of the period allocated for work on that particular project. The reason why I start with only 4 mins worth of BAing and gradually build up to 10 mins is because the start of the session, where group members are setting their aims and generally sorting themselves out, is unlike other phases in the group's work together and can be over quickly. If you spend an initial 10 mins with syndicate 1, then you might have missed out on the aim setting and planning phases in syndicate 2 altogether. For the same sorts of reasons I have found it unsatisfactory to spend 50 per cent of the time in one consecutive block with one group and then the remainder with the other. Also, I'm careful to switch over and spend my initial 4 mins with the other syndicate next time round.

Incidentally, all this dashing to and fro from group to group is very good for your figure – especially if the syndicate rooms are a fair distance apart, or even on different floors!

FEEDING BACK BEHAVIOURAL DATA

There isn't much point in dashing to and fro between groups, collecting tally marks on your improvised BA form, if you aren't going to put the data to some use. It may be that you have been collecting it in order to determine a new mixture of people into your groups which will better facilitate learning. If so, then the next section on mixing will be of especial interest to you. Even so, I don't advise you to skip this one entirely. If you are going to the trouble to assemble behavioural data, then you might as well get the best return you can for your efforts. The sort of return which I think perfectly feasible is to use the same basic behavioural data in two ways at least. One, to feedback to the course members in some form or another, and secondly, to use as a basis for making decisions about new groupings. So let's have a look at some starter ideas for feeding back behavioural information without the luxury of an operations room, computers and calculators.

I have used lots of 'do-it-yourself' strategies both for feeding back behavioural data to a group and for feeding back to individuals. The secret, not surprisingly, is that if you are on your own, then delegate as much as you can to the course members themselves.

For example, when pushed, I have simply handed my completed BA form, or forms, to the group, together with instructions about how to tot up the tally marks and interpret the data. This way I get the course members to do all the adding up, to calculate the totals into percentages and even to make up histogram displays or maintain a vast scoreboard on the blackboard or on flip chart paper pinned to a large wall. And it doesn't take long for seven or eight people in a group to process their own data like this. There is usually someone who is good with a slide rule and someone else who is a dab hand with the felt tip pens.

The range of visual displays for the data is literally vast and which you use very much depends upon your training objectives: there obviously isn't much point in producing fancy histograms in gay colours showing group behaviour during every work session if your objectives are all to do with individuals improving their interactive competence. This is why in ICL and BOAC group-oriented feedback gets minimal attention in relation to the individually oriented feedback. If, however, you are lucky enough to have a syndicate comprised of people who really do have to work together frequently as some sort of team on-the-job, then you may well use group-oriented and individually-oriented feedback as powerful devices to help you in achieving your objectives.

Another possibility is to use some group-oriented feedback as a stepping stone towards individually-oriented feedback. I have found that feeding back data about the group's behaviour is often an excellent way to warm people up to receiving data about their own behaviour. It is a great motivator in the sense that the group data seems, and indeed is, so impersonal to individual members of the group. OK, so the group has a high percentage of disagreeing. Is that because we have a couple of high disagreers or are we all equally responsible? As a result, people find group data rather tantalising and they start wanting to know the individual stuff very much indeed. **Getting them to want this sort of feedback is many times preferable to foisting it upon them.**

A couple of the more fancy displays you can go in for are blocks of colour on large sheets of graph paper representing the percentage proportion of behaviour falling into a particular BA category. Either you can put it all up this way or, of course, you may wish to highlight only certain of the categories you are using.

FIGURE 25 shows a histogram display I have often used.

Don't underestimate the amount of time it takes to produce this sort of display on your own. I once made the mistake of undertaking to produce histograms showing the behaviour over eight work sessions for four groups. It took me well into the night, kneeling on my hotel room floor, fiddling about with large sheets of graph paper and numerous felt tip pens! After that experience I learned to delegate!

25 histogram display

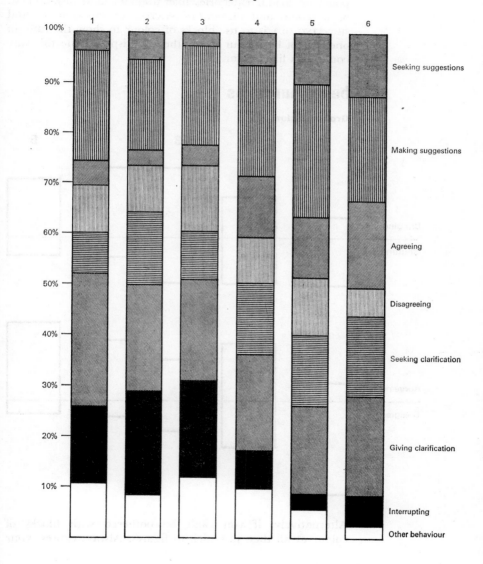

An alternative display which you can use if you are using poled behaviour categories like AGREEING and DISAGREEING or BUILDING and DIFFICULTY STATING or BRINGING IN and SHUTTING OUT is to use blocks of colour to show the ratio of one sort of behaviour to another. A display done this way could look like FIGURE 26.

26 behaviour ratios

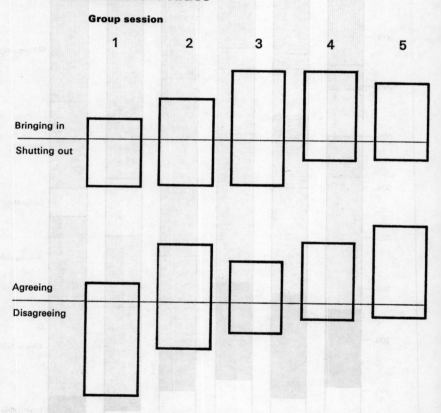

Alternatively, if you can't be bothered with blocks of colour at all then just stick to figures. Always express your raw data as percentages, though, so that comparisons of behaviour over a number of sessions – which will probably vary in length – are possible. If you do it this way, then the simplest thing to do is have a scoreboard where the percentages are entered at the conclusion of each work session. If you are single-handed and you want to indulge in individually-oriented feedback, then you are virtually forced – by the sheer amount of work – to get the individual to calculate his own percentages, using your raw data, and to get him to keep his own behavioural score-card. I have given individuals a duplicated sheet which they can use to keep a record of their feedback data session by session. I have even had the temerity to get them to do it in duplicate! One copy for them, one copy for me!

Which brings us to matters like the frequency of feedback sessions and the structuring of such sessions so that they are positive, helpful affairs rather than being destructive or just neutral, navel-contemplating periods.

The question of how often to feedback behavioural data clearly can't be answered by me in panacea-like terms. It clearly depends entirely on your training objectives. I have run courses where I have had a feedback session at the conclusion of every group work session or project. Assuming two projects per half day, then this can mean upwards of four sessions per day. Alternatively, I have had designs where this happened only once or twice a day. I'm sure that the important thing to grasp is that feedback sessions done properly take time. This is because it isn't just a question of singing out the figures to people and getting them to do some calculating and recording. The hallmark of a successful feedback session is that each individual understands the data and has formulated actionable plans or proposals for behavioural modifications or changes. (These words aren't synonymous for most people I find. Behavioural change is perceived as far more radical and, therefore, unlikely, than behavioural modifications!) So people must have time for the implications of the data to sink in. They must have time to make comparisons and discover the existence or non-existence of trends. And, above all, they must have time to decide what to do next using the data as their basis for reaching judgments and decisions. You have seen how these sessions are conducted in BOAC and in ICL. They are not ten minute affairs. In ICL individuals are given one whole hour to work on their own and then typically do some more behavioural planning immediately after this when they meet back in their groups. It takes the same length of time when the data which is being fedback spans a number (5, 6 or 7) of work sessions.

For all these reasons, I favour structured feedback sessions. By this I mean that the feedback should take place within the context of some individual or group project or task. You have seen some examples from the BOAC and ICL descriptions. Getting individuals to hand in a scrap of paper, or a form, with their fresh behavioural targets noted on it is a good way of forcing people to use the feedback as a basis for future action, rather than treating it solely as an interesting piece of historical data.

I suppose the other tip about indulging in feedback was exemplified very clearly in the earlier chapter on the subject.

**Don't play the expert
when dealing with
something as organic
as behavioural data**

That is, don't play the expert when dealing with something as organic as behavioural data. Remember that when feeding back information you are more a humble servant who happens to have been privileged enough to sit in on the groups at work and have had the sense to structure your observing opportunity. People will never really understand that different behaviour is appropriate to different situations if you railroad them with rights and wrongs, behavioural goodies and badies. I once made the mistake of giving a group some so-called ideal behavioural norms. They took the form of percentage proportions; 5 per cent of this, 10 per cent of that; not more than 15 per cent of the other. The group gobbled this up like starving men and I was horrified to see how influencial my norms were in all their future behavioural planning. They completely destroyed all original thought about different behaviours and how they are related to each other and different interactive situations. So my conclusion is to avoid being branded as an expert. Do your best to help people to interpret the data sensibly, help them to shape their own conclusions and proposals, but don't do it for them.

MIXING

Neil Rackham's chapter on mixing commends this technique to all trainers who use groups or syndicates as one of the means of achieving learning. His message is simple and its implications profound. He points out that, since the people we are with in any situation are enormously influential in shaping and affecting our behaviour, the same will hold good in training groups and syndicates. We have all heard people lament over the group they were in on a course. 'Unfortunately I was saddled with two noisy bs and couldn't get a word in edgeways.' 'Out of seven of us, four were from overseas and the language problem slowed us right down.' 'I got stuck in a group with a thick skinned know-all. It took us until Thursday to sort him out.'

Now it is easy to take such remarks with a pinch of salt and to shrug them off as inevitable. It is also easy to argue that the pot-luck involved in joining a randomly-selected group is in itself a good thing and absolutely deliberate. The argument goes that, since in real life we do get saddled with noisy bs, with foreigners and with know-alls, then it is quite OK to get saddled with them in the mini-culture of a course. But this assumes that real life and training situations are, or should be, as similar as possible. Whereas we all know that training situations and work situations are different. They always have different objectives and purposes, they frequently have a different means-end balance and they are usually differently contrived and structured.

Furthermore, I find it useful to hang on to the thought that **It is the trainer's job** it is the trainer's job to create a learning environment and **to create a learning** control it in such a way as to maximise the probability of the **environment and** learning objectives being achieved. Jeopardising this proba-**control it in such a** bility by knowingly permitting perhaps the most important **way as to maximise** single factor – the different people interacting in the situation **the probability of the** – to remain totally uncontrolled is, it seems to me, a serious **learning objectives** training crime. **being achieved** But enough of the moralising; let's look at the mixing techniques you can easily employ. As Neil Rackham showed, the simplest basis on which to mix people is on contribution levels. I have already shown that you can collect data about this in a very straightforward way by just putting a tally mark

beside the speaker's name at, say, 5-second intervals. So to do
this you don't need behaviour categories at all. You do need,
however, to do your contribution analysis covering a total
of at least 60 minutes' worth of interaction. And the best
interactive occasion is one where the group members are
about equal in terms of subject knowledge. In other words,
the task or project they are tackling should not be biased
strongly in favour of some and against others, since this will
obviously contaminate the contribution levels. You must feel
certain that the information you have collected about noisy
and quiet people is truly representative and reliable enough
to base firm predictions on.

Once you have assembled the data, then the rest is easy.
Tot up the tally mark totals. Put the names and totals into
rank order and see where the groupings come. For example,
here are some actual figures, already in rank order, on the
contribution levels of 12 people – in two different groups –
over a one hour period

Bill	229
Dave	202
Roger	198
Alan	187
Ken	150
Peter	110
Mike	108
Brian	79
Nigel	67
Neil	54
Fred	30
Chris	23

You now have to decide whether to split them into two
groups of six by drawing a line between Peter and Mike or
whether to include Mike in the high contributors' group or
Peter in the low contributors' group. What I did, in fact,
was to draw the line between Mike and Brian. This gave me
a group of high contributors seven strong and a group of low
contributors five strong. Since my objective was particularly
to aid the low contributors, this decision seemed the most
appropriate. Of course, the situation is helped if you have

more people – enough to make at least three groups rather than just two.

Alternative mixes obviously depend on what behaviour analysis categories you are using. I have found that putting high agreers together and high disagreers together is a good mixing strategy, as is separating the high seekers from the high givers. You can put the people who generate lots of ideas and proposals together in one group and the people who are more dependent on other people's ideas in another. Another useful refinement of the seeker/giver theme is to divide the givers of clarification, the people who tend to recap and to summarise, from the seekers of clarification.

Whatever the actual behavioural basis for the mix, I find it useful to remember two things. Firstly, that the overall purpose in reconstituting the training groups is always to facilitate learning, never to mess people up or trick them out. Thus I have found that putting high disagreers together helps them to reduce this behaviour and find alternative behavioural strategies more significantly and more rapidly than if I hadn't engineered the group membership. Secondly, I find it is important to have a basis for mixing which is easily comprehended and appreciated by the course members themselves. Accordingly, I am always completely open about the basis for the mix. It is all discussed with them and it is worth noting that such a discussion is in itself an important bit of feedback. As a matter of fact, and this is back to my earlier point about being singlehanded and having to delegate, when I have felt that groups could cope with it, I have let them decide the basis for the mix. This involves furnishing them with the behavioural data gathered up to that point in time, telling them about the rationale for mixing and helping them to scan the data for significant behavioural groupings. Whenever I have done this I have found the participants' interest to be very high and commitment to the mixes and to the respective group's behavioural targets to be heightened also.

The frequency of mixes will depend on the nature of the work being undertaken by the groups, together with the extent to which you wish to achieve behavioural changes. BOAC and ICL mix about once every day on a five day programme. This gives a sensible period for the group to make progress and for diagnosis in preparation for the next mix. But if you are interested in using mixes to facilitate other learning through, say, case study work or business games, then you may want to mix less often. I hope that we have shown convincingly that if you mixed on contribution rates alone this would be infinitely preferable to doing nothing in this area.

CONCLUSION

Well, that's it. I have just about run out of starter suggestions for you. I think it is sensible to end on a serious note. Remember that any training activities which really set out to change people's behaviour are hot stuff. So hot in fact that some people aren't up to handling it. Accordingly I would remind you that we have been glad to give you a leg up into the interactive skills field, providing you undertake your tasks in a responsible and diligent fashion. Please don't think me too patronising if I refer you back to the code of practice set out by Neil Rackham in the preceding chapter. ✳

NEIL RACKHAM

Graduated in Psychology from Sheffield University, staying there to do research in training evaluation. Joint author of the book *Evaluation of Management Training* 1970, and a number of more obstruse academic publications. Worked in organisation consultancy with the late William Allen and now divides his time between research, holding grants from BOAC and the Air Transport and Travel ITB for developing the interactive skills area, and other consultancy activities.

PETER HONEY

Peter Honey has a degree in psychology and is a founder member of the Division of Occupational Psychology in the British Psychological Society.

He started his industrial life as a job analyst with the Ford Motor Company and then moved to BOAC to advise their selection team on selection methods. He spent an academic year as senior lecturer in Occupational Psychology in the Management Department of Slough College, before specialising in the development of interactive skills with BOAC supervisors and junior managers.

He left BOAC in 1969 to become a self-employed management consultant, again specialising in the interactive skills field. He acts in this capacity for International Computers Limited, as well as for other organisations and has written extensively about his work.

MICHAEL J COLBERT

Michael Colbert read Industrial Relations and Economics at the University of Wales, then took a Dip.Ed., specialising in Adult Education. Taught for a time. Joined BEA in 1959 and held various training and education posts in the supervisory and management areas. Joined BOAC in 1966 and became Manager, General Training in 1967. He has encouraged behavioural science research into BOAC training methods and used the results to develop systematic data-based approaches to training problems.

RAY FIELDS

An engineer by training and trainer by choice – a choice based upon his experience and progress within the television, engineering and food industries. His first awareness of interactive skills at work came during his term of office as shop steward in a television union. Later, working as Personnel and Training Manager to a Scottish engineering group he had ample opportunity to explore his ideas of working with people more effectively. One result of his activities was the breaking down of communication barriers within the works for which he was responsible. When he was appointed Group Training Manager in the Cerebos Foods group of companies he came into contact with the now familiar activity of Management by Objectives. An important aspect of his role was providing supportive training to the individual M by O advisers and to the unit action groups. He joined the ICL management training team in 1969 and is now a Director of Studies.

DEREK HINSON

Graduated in Geography from Liverpool University. He started his career as a teacher, gaining experience in a university, the Army, and a grammar school before moving into industrial training. During the past 12 years he has worked in three major industries – iron and steel, printing and paper packaging, and now civil aviation – and has been involved in a wide range of training activities. His main areas of interest have been supervisory and middle management training and operative training. He joined BOAC in 1969 having been attracted by the early developments in interactive skills training.

TERRY MORGAN

Secondary education at Weymouth Grammar School. Obtained BSc Special in Physics at Kings College London, 1960. Then read Psychology at University College London before moving to Birkbeck College for postgraduate training in Occupational Psychology. From 1963-66 was a member of the research staff of the Department of Occupational Psychology, Birkbeck College, and with Professor Alec

Rodger carried out an investigation of the work of industrial training officers. Awarded Master of Philosophy degree from the University of London for thesis – *A Study of the Work of Industrial Training Officers* – derived from this research. In 1966, moved to BOAC, where he was responsible for personnel research. Helped to initiate the research into interactive skills which is the subject of this book. Joined the Air Transport and Travel ITB as Research Adviser in March 1969. Responsible for advising the Board on all matters relating to research and manpower planning in the industry. Current interests (besides interactive skills training) include occupational classification, manpower forecasting, instructional/learning models, and – inevitably – the selection and training of training staff.

MICHAEL MORRIS

After taking a degree in English at Oxford, he trained and worked as a specialist in language training in Madrid and Istanbul. In 1965 he joined BEA as Education Officer and subsequently took over the company's large-scale administrative training scheme. In 1967 he went to BOAC to set up and run administrative and graduate training schemes, but soon turned most of his attention to management training.
It was in this area that he and Peter Honey pioneered their new approach to interactive skills training for managers, starting the development that has led to the current sophisticated product. Although these activities have taken up a great deal of his time, he has also developed work and manages a small training team in ICL, where he is currently working as a Director of Studies, Management Training.

ROGER SUGDEN

Graduated in Psychology and Philosophy at Sheffield University. Taking a year off from formal studies to act as secretary to the Students' Union gave him the opportunity to carry out research into the objectives of teaching methods in higher education with the National Union of Students. The results of this study were briefly tested during a short spell as a lecturer in further education. He left academic education to join Neil Rackham and Peter Honey in their work with industry in 1969, where he has worked primarily on needs analysis, diagnostics and behaviour training.

STEPHEN TRIBE

Originally a chemist – graduating from Birmingham University in 1964. Conversion to social science – specifically organisation theory – occurred while he was attending the Principles of Industrial Management course at Cambridge. From 1965 to early 1969 he was BEA Management Studies Research Fellow, while attached to Imperial College's Management Engineering Department. The research involved studies both of the syndicate activity of people attending management training courses and of managers in the working situation. Between concluding the fieldwork for the research and joining BOAC as training development officer in October 1970, he was a training consultant, specifically engaged in industrial relations and in a group development project.

He is about to submit his doctoral thesis – *Structure and Activity of Task Directed Groups*.

The chapters of this book were published originally as separate articles in the monthly journal
INDUSTRIAL AND COMMERCIAL TRAINING.

As a result, this journal will become one of the most important organs of communication in the interactive area of training for management skills. Comment on the series is to be expected; contributors may be expected to write about their experiences in applying the concepts within their own organisations; some criticism is inevitable. Already there have been requests for more light to be shed on certain aspects of the technique.

One interesting feature to follow as it develops will be the way in which the DIS concepts are adapted for use in a wide variety of interactive situations. For instance, a psychologist is interested in using the concepts in the training of marriage guidance counsellors. A personnel specialist is interested in applying the techniques to selection, recruitment and placement in order to bring about an improved behaviour match between the job and the incumbent. Predictably there is great interest in the use of DIS techniques in the training of salesmen.

These developments will be reported, as they take place, in
INDUSTRIAL AND COMMERCIAL TRAINING.

The journal appears monthly and costs £5.00 per annum, postage included, from
WELLENS PUBLISHING
Guilsborough, Northampton NN6 8PY, England
Telephone: 060-122 379

A

Action Centred Leadership 48
Action Skill, as T group goal 23, 44
Affiliation needs 6
Air Transport & Travel ITB 38, 63
Allen, W W 71-2, 75, 80
Analysis of
— behaviour survey data 77-84
— group behaviour data 123
— individual behaviour data 123-30
Appraisal systems 119
Argyle, M 4-5, 6, 14, 25, 44
Argyris, C 22-3
Atomic Energy Research Establishment
162
Attitudes
— changes in 4, 10
— effect of case studies on 15
— relation of to behaviour 4, 8-10, 69

B

Bales, R F 49
— inadequacies of Bales interaction
analysis 49, 57-8, 95
Behaviour
— non-verbal components of 5, 169
— relation of attitude change to 4, 9-12
— relation of to skills 7, 11
Behaviour aims worksheet 137-8
Behaviour Analysis
— and group effectiveness 69-74
— and individual categories *see*
behaviour categories
— and organisational effectiveness
74-91
— computer processing of 122
— criteria for categories 95-6
— development of 57-8
— initial practice with 169
— range of categories used 169-71
— time sampling methods for 171
— training observers for 113-7
— use of in meetings 167
— with restricted resources 162, 172-3
Behaviour categories 96-7
— range used in DIS development
169-71
— specificity of 86
— criteria for 95-6
— *building* 79, 100-1
— *caught proposals* 100
— *clarifying* 104
— *confusing* 105
— *criticising* 79

— *escaped proposals* 100
— *multi-speak* 101
— *offering explanations* 101
— *talking over* 105
— *testing understanding* 102
Behaviour change and group
composition 49, 145-153
Behaviour surveys
— cluster analyses of 81-4
— in BOAC 77-84
— in ICL 84-8
— involvement of managers in 84-6
Behavioural experimentation as a
vehicle for attitude change 12
Blake, R R 27-31, 32-35, 40-1, 44
Blake's Grid 31-35, 36, 54
Building behaviour 79, 100-1

C

Campbell et al 25, 41, 44
Canada, effectiveness clusters in 77-9
Case studies as a training method 15-16
Check lists in IT training 28
Classification systems for interactive
skills 6
Cluster analysis of organisation
behaviour 81-4
Code of practice in DIS 159-60
Composition of groups *see* mixing
Computer processing of behaviour
analysis 122
Contribution rate mixes 149-156
Coverdale, R 35, 44, 146
Coverdale Training 35-9, 48
— goals of 36
— limitations of 38-9
— systematic approach in 36
Criteria for DIS development 50
Critical incident technique in training
needs analysis 52
— compared with job description
technique 52
Criticising behaviour 79
Cultural values 80-91
— comparison of USA and UK 80-4
Cybernetic view of performance
improvement 57

D

Data processing load in DIS 61-2, 174
Diagnostic ability, as T group goal 23
Diagnostic stage of DIS 59
Discovery learning in skilled
performance 13-14

Drives, social 6
Dyad interactions 7-8, 171

E
Effectiveness of behaviour patterns
chapter 3
 — getting a 'feel' for 164
 — in BOAC 77-84
 — in ICL 85-88
Ego identity 6
Empathy in dyad interaction 8
Esso Petroleum 35
Ethical problems in DIS 55-6
Evaluation
 — in DIS training 94
 — in relation to research 51
 — lack of in interactive skills area 12-13
 — short and long cycle systems 59-63

F
Fawley blue book 71
Feedback
 — in appraisal systems 119
 — in DIS training 57-61
 — in interview situations 120
 — in T groups 26
 — long cycle 63
 — of behavioural data chapter 3, 94
 — role of in developing skilled
performance 13
 — short cycle 59-63
 — strategies of 173-8
 — using limited resources 162, 172-3
Fishbein & Ajzen 69
Frequency analysis 171

G
Goal obsession in interactive skills
training 54
Golden rule fallacy 53
Grid, Managerial 31-5
Group dynamics, history of 19-20
Group method in interactive skills
training 18-20
Group morale and productivity 18
Groups
 — and organisational function 18
 — composition of *see* mixing
 — effectiveness of and individual
performance 69-74
 — influence of on individual behaviour
145

H
Hall, J 28, 30, 45

Hawthorne effect in team training 41
Hawthorne Studies 18
Haynes Task Centred Analysis 95
Honey, P 48-9, 50, 56, 62
House, R J 24, 44
Human relations 1-2
Human skills 4

I
Innovative style of management 134-5
Instrumented Laboratory Training 26-31
 — check lists in 28
 — ranking procedures in 28
 — rating scales in 27-8
Interactive behaviour
 — definition of 73
 — relation of to organisational
effectiveness 74-91
Interactive skills
 — code of practice for 159-60
 — definition of 4
 — need for taxonomy in 5
 — role of discovery learning in 13-14
 — traditional methods for training in 15
 — varieties of 14
Interface behaviour chapter 3
 — importance of 73-4
 — organisational status and 74
Intervention strategies
 — disadvantages of 49, 110
 — guidelines for in IT training 29

J
Job description
 — comparison of with critical incident
technique 52
 — inadequacy of for training needs
analysis 52

K
Knowledge
 — cultural differences in 82-3
 — relation to skills 2

L
Laboratory training 21
 — Instrumented form of 26-31
Leadership, Ohio studies of 77
Learning, group dependent factors in 147
Lewin, Kurt 19
Line management, involvement of in
organisation behaviour surveys 84-6
Long-cycle feedback in DIS 63

M

Maier & Zerfoss 16, 44
Management by Objectives and key behaviours 168
Management consultants, sensitivity of to micro-cultures 75
Management, interactive component in 52, 73-4
Management succession 89
Managerial grid 31-5
Managerial styles 134-5
Managers, reactions of to DIS 141-2
Meetings as source of behavioural data 167
Micro-cultures
— behavioural consequences of 72
— consultant's role with 75
— measurement of 76-91
Mixing of groups chapter 6, 58, 179-82
— contribution rate 149-56
— negative behaviour mixes 57-81
— variables influencing outcome of 156
Models
— of trainer function 61-2
— of typical DIS course 64-5
Motivators, social 6
Mouton, Jane S 27-31, 32-5, 45
Multiple role playing 16-18

N

Negative behaviour mixes 157-8
Non-verbal behaviour 5, 169

O

Odiorne, George S 25, 44
Ohio leadership studies 77
Open styles of management 134-5
Operations room 61-2, 121
Organisation Development 69, 84, 89-91
Organisational behaviour
— cluster analysis of 81-4
— problems of describing 70
— survey methods in 76-91
Organisational climate
— determinants of 71
— measurement of 76-91
— relation of to organisational behaviour 72-6
— relation of to promotion channel 89
Organisational effectiveness
— and individual performance 74-91
— involvement of management in assessing 84-6
— role of top management in 71

P

Participative style of management 134-5
Perceptions, low correlation of with behavioural measures 49
Performance improvement through feedback 57
Practice as a necessity for skilled performance 13
Productivity and group morale 18
Promotion channels 89
Protestant ethic, behaviour cluster of 83-4
Psychodrama 16-17

Q

Questionnaire formats for behaviour surveys 165

R

Rackham, Neil 69, 95, 139, 179
Ranking procedures in IT training 28
Rating procedures in IT training 27-8
Relevance
— as criterion for job carry-over 50
— compared with compatability of training values 80-1
Reliability of observation 109
Research, role of in DIS development 51
Resourcing problems of DIS 162
Roche, Seamus 35, 45
Role playing 16-18

S

Semantic differential perceptual measures 61
Sensitivity, as a T group goal 23
Sensitivity training 21
Sequence analysis of behavioural data 112
Session assessment questionnaires 123, 129-30
Sheffield University Evaluation Unit 49
Short-cycle feedback 59-63
Skilled performance
— discovery learning in 13-14
— practice of 13
— relation of feedback to 13
Skills, relation of to attitudes 9-11
Smith, Peter 20, 23-24, 44
Smith, Stuart 77
Social drives 6
Social motivators 6
Social sensitivity 8
Social skills, definition of 4

Social techniques 5
Solem, A R 17, 44
Statistical tests for behaviour surveys 77
Styles of management 134-5
Supervision
 — effective behaviour of in UK BOAC 76
 — effective behaviour of in USA 80-4
 — interactive component in 52
Supportive style of management 134-5
Syndicate groups, application of DIS to
  48, 179-81
Systematic approach, in Coverdale
  training 36

T
T Groups
 — feedback in 26, 57
 — goals of 22-3
 — methods 20-31, 96
 — reaction of managers to 57
 — relation to job performance 23-4
 — risks of 144-5, 147
 — trainers role in 21-2, 26
Task orientation in Grid training 31
Team training 39-41
Time sampling of behaviour 171
Top management and organisational
  performance 71
Trainer's role
 — in DIS 60-3, 110

 — in IT training 29-30
 — in T groups 21-2, 26
Training in Behaviour analysis 113-116
Training needs analysis
 — inadequacy of Job Description
techniques 52
 — use of Critical Incident techniques in
52
Training, value systems of 80-1

U
USA
 — and Protestant Ethic 84
 — application of knowledge in 82-3
 — cultural values in 81-4
 — effective behaviours in 77-84

V
Value systems
 — of organisations chapter 3
 — of training 79-81
Video tape, use of
 — in category development 49, 57-8
 — in observer training 113-6

W
Warr, Bird & Rackham 63
Western Electric Co 18
Whitaker, G 20, 44

Modal techniques 5
power, the 17, 18
Situational tests for behaviour surveys 77
Skilled management 154-5
supervision
— effective behaviour of in UK BOAC 78
— effective behaviour of in USA OC 77
— unpersuasive component in 8...
Supportive style of management 134-6
Supply and demand, analysis of DIS 127,
59, 173-81
Systematic approach to
training 58

T
the top
— feedback in 24, 37
— role of 22-3
— methods 20, 37, 99
— reaction of managers to 67
— relation to job performance 23-4
— roles of 134-5, 147
2 anticipation 21, 2, 28
Task identification in OnE training 31
Team training 31, 41
Three-phase plan of behaviour 174
Top management and organisational
performance 21
trainer's role
— in DIS 59-62, 175
— in IT training 29, 30
— in T groups 31-2, 36
Training in behaviour analysis 14-3-116
training needs analysis
— inadequacy of Job Description
techniques 62
— use of Critical Incident techniques in
62
Training value systems of 90-1

U
USA,
— and Prospect of Ohio 94
— application of knowledge in 82-3
— cultural values in 81-4
— effective behaviour in 72-8, 81

V
value systems
— of supermarket chapter 3
Video, team use of
— 4 training 29, 31
— in laboratory development 43, 57-8
— in observer training 113-6

W
Warr, Bird & Rackham 62
Wellens Ltd, the 12-13
Whitelaw, G 20, 44